Learn to Spell 500 Words a Day: The Vowel O [vol. 4]

The Vowel **O** has **12** sounds we call phonics, which are spelled in **20** ways we call spelling patterns.

How to Use this Book V

Section 1: The Long ō Sound 1
Long ō spelled in nine ways: Mell**ow**, C**ou**rtney, J**oe**, J**oa**n, R**o**se, Plat**o**, S**ol**dier, R**oy**, Detr**oi**t

1 ōw

Chapter 1: The long ō sound spelled with "**ow**" as in "Mell**ow**"

Lesson 1: Meaning of a Long Vowel 3
Lesson 2: The Homonyms' Theory 4
Lesson 3: The "**ōw**" phonic in **129** words 5
Lesson 4: The "**ōw**" words in a story about "Mell**ow**" 7
Homework 9

2 ōu

Chapter 2: The long ō sound spelled with "**ou**" as in "C**ou**rtney"

Lesson 1: Meaning of a Long Vowel 11
Lesson 2: The two vowels walking Rule 12
Lesson 3: The "**ōu**" phonic in **39** words 13
Lesson 4: The "**ōu**" words in a story about "C**ou**rtney" 14
Homework 15

3 ōe

Chapter 3: The long ō sound spelled with "**oe**" as in "J**oe**"

Lesson 1: Meaning of a Long Vowel 17
Lesson 2: The two vowels walking Rule 18
Lesson 3: The "**ōe**" phonic in **24** words 19
Lesson 4: The "**ōe**" words in a story about "J**oe**" 20
Homework 21

4 ōa

Chapter 4: The long ō sound spelled with "**oa**" as in "J**oa**n"

Lesson 1: Meaning of a Long Vowel 23
Lesson 2: The two vowels walking Rule 24
Lesson 3: The "**ōa**" phonic in **144** words 25
Lesson 4: The "**ōa**" words in a story about "J**oa**n" 28
Homework 30

I

Chapter 5: The long ō sound spelled with "o-e" as in "Rose"

Lesson 1: Meaning of a Long Vowel	31
Lesson 2: The "ō-e" Rule	32
Lesson 3: The "ō-e" phonic in **267** words	33
Lesson 4: A list of **57** r-controlled words as in "St**ore**"	40
Lesson 5: The r-controlled words in a story about a "St**ore**keeper"	41
Lesson 6: Spelled like long ō but not long ō, as in "gl**ove**"	42
Lesson 7: The "ō-e" words in a story about "R**ose**"	43
Homework	52

Chapter 6: The long ō sound spelled with "o" as in "Plato"

Lesson 1: Meaning of a Long Vowel	55
Lesson 2: The stressed final "o´" Rule	56
Lesson 3: The "o´" phonic in **133** words	57
Lesson 4: The "o´" words in a story about "Plat**o´**"	59
Homework	61

Chapter 7: The long ō sound spelled with "o + semivowel" as in "Soldier"

Lesson 1: Meaning of a Long Vowel	63
Lesson 2: The "o + semivowel" Rule	64
Lesson 3: The "ō + semivowel" phonic in **49** words	65
Lesson 4: The "ō + semivowel" words in a story about a "S**ol**dier"	67
Lesson 5: The "**or**" as in "b**or**n"	69
Lesson 6: The "**or**" phonic in **85** words	69
Lesson 7: The "**or**" words in a story about "Elean**or**"	71
Homework	74

Chapter 8: The long ō sound spelled with "ōy" as in "Roy"

Lesson 1: Meaning of a Long Vowel	77
Lesson 2: The "ōy" as in "b**oy**" at end of words	78
Lesson 3: The "ōy" phonic in **63** words	79

Contents of the Vowel O

Lesson 4: The "ōy" words in a story about "Roy"	80
Homework	81

9 ōi — Chapter 9: The long ōi sound spelled with "oi" as in "Detroit"

Lesson 1: Meaning of a Long Vowel	83
Lesson 2: The "ōi" as in "boil" for inside words	84
Lesson 3: The "ōi" phonic in **102** words	85
Lesson 4: The "ōi" words in a story about "Detroit"	87
Homework	89

Section 2: The Short ŏ Sound
The short ŏ sound followed by one or two consonant as in "hot" and "hotter." — 91

10 ŏ — Chapter 10: The short ŏ sound as in "Ron"

Lesson 1: Meaning of a Short Vowel	93
Lesson 2: The short vowels' Rule	94
Lesson 3: The short ŏ phonic in **182** words	95
Lesson 4: The short ŏ words in a story about "Ron"	99
Lesson 5: The pronunciations of "o + semivowel" vary as in "long"	100
Lesson 6: Compare short ŏ with long ō	101
Homework	103

Section 3: Nine Other Sounds of O — 105
Cowboy, Counselor, Snoopy, Goode, Ought to, Who, Lou, Renoir, Doug

11 OW — Chapter 11: The "ow" sound as in "Cowboy"

Lesson 1: The "ow" as in "cow" for the end of words	107
Lesson 2: The "ow" phonic in **102** words	108
Lesson 3: The "ow" words in a story about a "Cowboy"	110
Homework	112

12 OU=OW — Chapter 12: The "ou" as in "Counselor"

Lesson 1: The "ou" as in "out" for inside words	113
Lesson 2: The "ou" phonic in **108** words	114
Lesson 3: The "ou" words in a story about a "Counselor"	116

Chapter 13: The "oo" sound as in "Snoopy"

Homework	118
Lesson 1: The "oo" as in "too"	119
Lesson 2: The "oo" phonic in **137** words	120
Lesson 3: The "oo" words in a story about "Snoopy"	123
Homework	125

Chapter 14: The "oo" sound as in "Ms. Goode"

Lesson 1: The "oo" as in "good"	127
Lesson 2: The "oo" phonic in **28** words	128
Lesson 3: The "oo" words in a story about "Ms. Goode"	129
Homework	130

Chapter 15: **Five** minor sounds of "o": Ought, Who, Lou, Renoir, Doug

Lesson 1: The "**Ou**" as in "**Ou**ght to"	132
Lesson 2: The one "**o**" as in "Wh**o**"	133
Lesson 3: The "**ou**" as in "L**ou**"	134
Lesson 4: The "**o**" says "**w**" as in "Ren**o**ir"	135
Lesson 5: The silent "**o**" as in "D**o**ug"	136
Homework	137

Section 4: The weak sound of "o" called a schwa sound — 139

Chapter 16: The schwa sounds of "o" as in "Professor"

Lesson 1: Meaning of a Schwa ə	141
Lesson 2: The schwa sound of "**o**" in **70** words	142
Lesson 3: The schwa ə sound of "**o**" in a story about a "Profess**o**r"	143
Homework	144

About the author and about other phonics-based spelling books by Camilia Sadik — 145

How to Use this Book

Italic letters in this book represent silent letters, like the silent *p* in recei*p*t.

Dots inside words indicate divisions of words into syllables, as in win·dow.

Vowels are **a**, **e**, **i**, **o**, **u**, sometimes **y** as in sk**y** and sometimes **w** as in fe**w**. Vowels rule English and they cannot be avoided. Vowels change drastically; they make **38** sounds we call phonics, which are spelled in **96** ways we call spelling patterns. To learn all the changes in the vowels, an entire book is written to teach each vowel.

Consonants are the rest of the letters. Vowels are very inconsistent and the eight consonants c, g, h, q, s, x, w, and y are also inconsistent. The eight inconsistent consonants are isolated in a book; they produce **50** sounds, which are spelled in **60** ways.

A syllable is a part of a word, like "me" in "me·di·a" or it is a word, like "me" that contains only one vowel sound. There are two syllables in "win·dow." There are five syllables in "com·mu·ni·ca·tion." There are three syllables in "beau·ti·ful." There is one syllable in "stopp*e*d." A syllable may contain more than one vowel but it can only have one vowel sound. Read more in the *Teachers' Guide*.

A schwa is a weak sound of any vowel, as in sep·**a**·rate, sou·v**e**·nir, sol·**i**·tude, mem·**o**·ry, and vir·**u**s. Other syllables may be stressed, but not the syllables where the schwa is.

A phonic is a single sound produced by a number of letters (**ture** in cul·**ture**) or by a letter that does not sound like its letter name (**y** in sk**y**).

Semivowels l, m, n, r, and s: Vowels have sounds and consonants are soundless unless they are said with a vowel. In spite of being consonants, the l, m, n, r, and s have some sounds of their own, even when not said with vowels. Moreover, these five consonants have various effects on the vowels that precede them; and sometimes, they act like vowels. They may make the preceding vowels long, as in ch**il**d, c**om**b, r**an**ge, p**or**t, and p**as**te. For this reason, the author granted the name semivowels to these five consonants.

Reading aloud is imperative and there are details about reading aloud in the *Teachers' Guide*. Learners must read aloud all the practice lessons in these books. If reading silently, students may understand but will not memorize the spelling of words.

Logical Learners: English words were not written for logical learners who need logic before they can memorize. In English, one needs to memorize without logic which spelling pattern of a sound to choose when spelling every single sound in every English word. Logical learners are analyzers who question the logic behind spelling English words one-way and not the other. They simply cannot memorize without logical spelling rules to show them when to spell a sound one-way and not the other.

Dyslexic persons are logical learners; they need logical spelling rules before they can memorize the spelling of words. However, dyslexia in spelling and in writing letters in reverse does end, after learning to spell and after slowing down to write words slowly.

Typically, dyslexic persons are highly focused on one thing at a time; they cannot focus both on comprehension and on the way, words are spelled. While teachers may think, every child in the classroom is reading a story and looking for the main idea, kids who are logical learners are pausing to question, "Why My cat is cute isn't Mi kat iz qut?" Questioning causes them to fall behind, and then they are labeled with dyslexia.

Understanding dyslexia is the key to ending it. After reading, "How do you get dyslexia?" by Camilia Sadik, you will agree that dyslexia is given to kids before the 3rd grade. Forced speed-reading before learning to spell words causes dyslexia. When kids are forced to hurry, their vision travels rapidly from left-to-right and vice versa. In their haste, they see letters in reverse. When writing, they also hurry and write letters in reverse, in the same manner that they saw them and read them.

ADD can End: Most cases of ADD are due to boredom from sitting in class and not learning. When dyslexia ends so does ADD that is caused by dyslexia.

ESL students learn to speak, read, spell, write, and become literate in English in 400 to 500 hours of studying or supervised instructions, depending on their levels. At the start, they specifically benefit from *Read Instantly* and from *English for Non-native English Speakers*. At a later stage, they benefit from the rest of the books. ESL students can learn to read from *Read Instantly* even if they do not speak English; they read phonics similar to the way they read the ABC's.

Sadik's books are for all ages and all types of learners. All benefit from these comprehensive phonics-based reading and spelling books. They are ideal books for K-12 parents or teachers and for adult learners from diverse backgrounds. For sample lessons and much more, visit us at SpellingRules.com

Section 1: The Long ō Sound

The first sound of the vowel "o" is the long **ō** sound, and it is spelled in these **nine** ways: Mell**ow**, C**ou**rtney, J**oe**, J**oa**n, R**o**se, Plat**o**, S**ol**dier, R**oy**, and Detr**oi**t

Mellow

Courtney

Joe

Joan

Rose

Plato

Soldier

Roy

Detroit
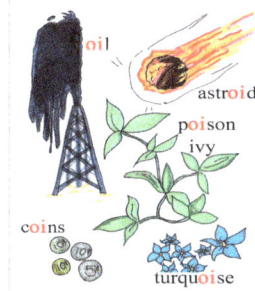

The long ō sound is spelled in these nine spelling patterns:

Chapter 1: "ow" as in "Mellow" — 3

Chapter 2: "ou" as in "Courtney" — 11

Chapter 3: "oe" as in "Joe" — 17

Chapter 4: "oa" as in "Joan" — 23

Chapter 5: "o-e" as in "Rose" — 31

Chapter 6: "o" as in "Plato" — 55

Chapter 7: "o + semivowel" as in "Soldier" — 63

Chapter 8: "oy" as in "Roy" — 77

Chapter 9: "oi" as in "Detroit" — 83

Chapter 1: Long ō - Mellow

Chapter 1: The long ō sound spelled with "ow" as in "Mellow"

1 ōw...low The first way to spell the long ō sound is with the "ow" phonic as in "low."

Lesson 1: Meaning of a Long Vowel

Memorize: Long "o" sounds like the name of the letter **O**.

The "o" is said to have a long sound when it sounds like the name of the letter **O**. The "ow" in "sow" sounds like the name of the letter **O** and that makes it a long ō.

The words "sow" and "so" sound alike but they have different meanings—words that sound the same but have different meanings are called homonyms. Without the "w," after the "o" in "sow," we would have the word "so," which has a different meaning.

Compare these homonyms of long ō:

know, no	throw, throe	thrown, throne
row, roe	sow, so	tow, toe
towed, toad	bowl, boll	slow, sloe
mow, Moe	owed, ode	knows, nose

Lesson 2: The Homonyms' Theory

throw or throe

Compare "thr**ow**" with "thr**oe**," and notice how the people who developed written English tried to use different spelling patterns for words that sounded the same but had different meanings (homonyms). ==They did that to tell apart two words, like "thr**ow**" and "thr**oe**," and once a new pattern was used to tell apart any two words, more words ended up being spelled with it.==

ōw...throw Similar to the final "ey" in "mon**ey**" wherein the "y" stops being a consonant and turns into a vowel, the final "w" in "**ow**" as in "thr**ow**" also stops being a consonant and turns into a vowel. Primarily, this "**ow**" pattern is for the end of words and the "ou" as in "s**ou**l" is for inside words.

Chapter 1: Long ō - Mellow

**Lesson 3:** The "ōw" phonic in 129 words (20 one-syllable words)

Read aloud slowly: Read aloud to memorize the spelling of words. Reading silently means using fewer senses; you memorize when you see the word, hear the word, and feel the word in your mouth as you utter it. Read slowly to see the way words are spelled and to avoid seeing letters in reverse. Avoid speed-reading before learning to spell words. If in a classroom, students need to read aloud together in one rhythm. The first 20 words below are one-syllable words meant to help beginners:

low	slow	flow	blow	glow	tow	stow
row	grow	throw	crow	bow	snow	know
mow	sow	show	owe	own	bowl	

snow	snows	snowed
snow·ing	know	knows
know·ing	known	un·known
low	low·er	low·est
slow	slow·er	slow·est
flow	flows	flown
blow	blows	blown
glow	glows	glowed
glow·ing	yel·low	yel·low·ish
fel·low	fel·lows	mel·low
mel·low·er	be·low	bel·low
bel·lows	bel·lowed	bel·low·ing
bil·low	bil·lows	bil·lowed
pil·low	pil·lows	wil·low
fol·low	fol·lowed	hol·low
sal·low	shal·low	shal·low·er
shal·low·est	wal·low	wal·lowed

5

tow	tows	towed
tow·ing	stow	stows
stowed	stow·ing	row
rows	grow	grown
in·grown	grows	growth
throw	thrown	throws
crow	scare·crow	bow
rain·bow	win·dow	shad·ow
mead·ow	lawn·mower	mow
mows	mowed	mow·ing
sow	sown	sows
sowed	sow·ing	show
shown	shows	showed
show·ing	owe	owes
owed	ow·ing	own
owns	owned	own·ing
own·er	home·owner	bowl
bowls	bowled	bowl·ing
to·mor·row	sor·row	bor·row
bor·rows	bor·row·er	bor·rowed
bor·row·ing	bur·row	bar·row
wheel·barrow	nar·row	ar·row
ar·rows	mar·row	spar·row

Chapter 1: Long ō - Mellow

Lesson 4: The "ōw" words in a story about "Mellow"

The name "Mellow" is chosen because it contains the "ow" phonic, and learners remember the spelling of the words that contain "ow" by associating them with "Mellow" in this series of sentences (this nonsensical story). Such stories may or may not make much sense, and their chief purpose is for remembering the spelling of words in one story (one context).

Read the following series of sentences (nonsensical story) aloud slowly:

Mel·low watched the rain·bow glow through his win·dow. Mel·low en·joyed see·ing the snow cov·er·ing the mead·ow. Mel·low felt a flow of en·er·gy and was read·y to blow out his birth·day can·dles a·mong his fam·i·ly and friends.

Mel·low wore his yel·low out·fit and pushed his wheel·barrow in·to the nar·row al·ley. Mel·low mowed the lawn us·ing an old lawn·mower, and then he de·cid·ed it was time to throw a·way his old lawn·mower. Mel·low need·ed to bor·row some mon·ey to buy a brand-new lawn·mower. Mel·low felt sor·row for hav·ing to bor·row mon·ey. Mel·low filled out a loan ap·pli·ca·tion and he was ap·proved to bor·row the mon·ey to·mor·row. Mel·low end·ed up hav·ing low self-esteem for hav·ing to owe mon·ey, and he need·ed to mel·low down. Mel·low owned his own home, so he was a home·owner.

Mel·low was a nice fel·low. Mel·low was a mel·low per·son. Mel·low's most re·cent grades were be·low av·er·age.

Mel·low re·gret·ted not fol·low·ing the in·struc·tions while stud·y·ing. Mel·low did not know he need·ed to read a·loud slow·ly. Mel·low was not a shal·low per·son. Mel·low's skin col·or looked sal·low a·fter swal·low·ing his food. Luck·i·ly, Mel·low did not need a bone mar·row trans·plant. Mel·low had been wal·low·ing in self-pity. Mel·low did know that to·mor·row would be a bet·ter day.

Mel·low went bowl·ing. Mel·low went to a show and sat in the front row. Mel·low's car was to be towed a·way. Mel·low said, "Grow·ing up is hard to do." Mel·low de·cid·ed to go to the farm. Mel·low sowed some veg·e·ta·ble seeds and watched them grow.

Mel·low fol·lowed that ar·row sign to those hol·low pil·lars. Mel·low slept with·out a pil·low un·der the wil·low tree. Mel·low heard the bull's bel·low. As the smoke bil·lowed from the fire, Mel·low ran and left his pil·low un·der the wil·low tree. Mel·low said,

"To bor·row means to re·ceive a loan, as in to bor·row mon·ey."
"A bar·row is as in a wheel·barrow that is pushed man·u·al·ly."

Chapter 1: Long ō - Mellow

"A b**ur**·**r**o**w** is a hol*e* in the ground, as in a rab·bit dug a b**ur**·**r**o**w**."

"A b**ur**·**r**o is a small don·key."

"A b**or**·**ough** is a self-govern*e*d town, as in the b**or**·**ough** of Man·hat·tan."

Copy these words and do not try to guess their spelling. Look at each word before you begin to copy it and do not look away from it until you are 100% confident that you can spell it:

borrow	barrow	burrow	burro
borough	snow	know	low
slow	flow	flown	blow
blown	glow	below	bellow
willow	pillow	yellow	mellow
fellow	follow	hollow	sallow
wallow	tow	towed	towing
stow	row	grow	grown
ingrown	growth	crow	scarecrow
bow	rainbow	window	shadow

9

meadow	mow	mowing	lawnmower
showing	owing	sow	sown
show	shown	owe	owing
own	owning	bowl	bowled
borrow	barrow	narrow	arrow
marrow	sparrow	slow	sloe
row	roe	throw	throe
thrown	throne	two	toe
towed	toad	know	no
owed	ode	mow	Moe
sow, so	sew	bowl, boll	knows, nose

Chapter 2: The long ō sound spelled with "ou" as in "Courtney"

The second way to spell the long ō sound is with "ou" as in "dough."

**Lesson 1:** Meaning of a Long Vowel

Memorize: The long "o" sounds like the name of the letter O.

Compare "Sol" with "soul." The "o" is said to have a long sound when it sounds like the name of the letter O. The "o" as in "soul" sounds like the name of the letter O and that makes it a long ō. The "o" in "Sol" does not sound like the name of the letter O. Without the silent "u," we would have "Sol" not "soul." The "o" in "Sol" has a unique short ŏ sound.

Perhaps this "ōu" spelling pattern of long ō was first used to tell apart homonyms like "soul" and "sole," and once the "ou" pattern was used, more words ended up being spelled with it.

Compare these homonyms:

soul, sole   pour, pore   your, yore

four, for   mould, mold   dough, doe

mourn·ing, morn·ing

Lesson 2: The two vowels walking Rule

Memorize: When two vowels are walking, the first one does the talking.

ōu...soul Compare "S**o**l" with "s**ou**l." As in "s**ou**l," when the two vowels "**o**" and "**u**" are next to each other (walking), the first one "**o**" does the talking and the second one "**u**" is silent. The first one "**o**" does the talking means it has a sound and that sound is a long sound, just like the name of the letter **O**. The silent "**u**" is there just to help the "**o**" say **O**. When we say that the "**o**" does the talking we mean the "**o**" is able to sound like the name of the letter **O**. Being able to say the name of the letter **O** means the "**o**" is long. Without the silent "**u**," we would have the word "S**o**l" not "s**ou**l."

Similarly, as in the syllable "p**ou**r´" in "p**ou**r´·ing," when "**o**" and "**u**" are next to each other in a stressed syllable, the "**o**" has the sound of the letter **O**, and the "**u**" is silent. Primarily, this "**ou**" pattern is for inside words and the "ow" as in "s**ow**" is for the end of words.

dough or doe

This "**ōu**" spelling pattern of long **ō** is useful to tell apart homonyms like "d**ou**gh" and "d**oe**."

Know that the two vowels walking rule applies only to two vowels that are in the same syllable and that syllable must be stressed. Furthermore, the rule applies only to specific two vowels, not to any two vowels next to one another. All such specific two vowels are made available in this book.

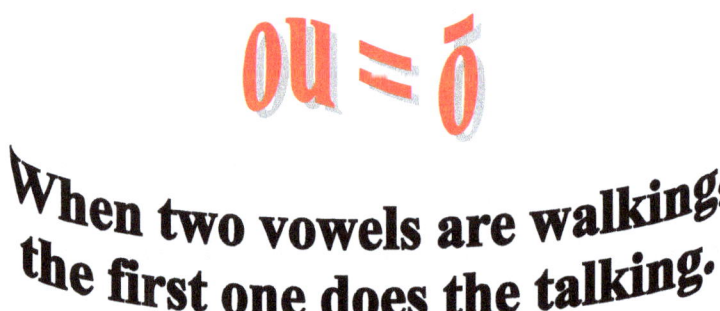

ōu = ō

When two vowels are walking, the first one does the talking.

Lesson 3: The "ō̄u" phonic is in approximately 39 useful words (11 one-syllable words)

Read aloud slowly:

soul	mould	source	course	four	your	pour
mourn	court	dough	though			

soul	souls	shoul·der
mould	course	cour·ses
of course	source	sour·ces
re·source	re·source·ful	four
your	pour	pours
poured	pour·ing	mourn
mourns	mourned	mourn·ing
court	court·house	court·yard
court·ly	Court·ney	bour·geois
bour·geoi·sie	bou·quet	dough
sour·dough	though	al·though
bor·ough	thor·ough	thor·ough·ly
fur·lough	fur·loughed	fur·lough·ing

**Lesson 4:** The "ōu" words in a story about "C**ou**rtney"

Read aloud slowly whether asked or not asked to do so:

Courtney C**ou**rt·ney was born in Franc*e*. C**ou**rt·ney's grand·parents were b**ou**r·g*eoi*·sies. C**ou**rt·ney was now a pet·ty b**ou**r·g*eois* liv·ing in the bor·**ou**g*h* of Man·hat·tan. C**ou**rt·ney sat at the c**ou**rt·yard, p**ou**red her·self a cup of cof·fee, and at*e* some s**ou**r·d**ou**g*h* bread.

C**ou**rt·ney took a f**ou**r-month c**ou**rs*e* to be·com*e* a par·a·le·gal. C**ou**rt·ney went to the c**ou**rt·hous*e* yes·ter·day to stud·y her grand·father's cas*e*. Al·th**ou**g*h* the de·tec·tiv*e*s were us·ing all their re·s**ou**r·ces to con·duct a thor·**ou**g*h* in·ves·ti·ga·tion a·bout his death, C**ou**rt·ney was not sat·is·fi*e*d with the re·sults. C**ou**rt·ney hir*e*d a pri·vat*e* in·ves·tiga·tor to re·v*ie*w all the s**ou**r·ces of this cas*e* thor·**ou**g*h*·ly.

C**ou**rt·ney had broad sh**ou**l·ders. C**ou**rt·ney act*e*d in a c**ou**rt·ly man·ner. C**ou**rt·ney took a b**ou**·q*u*et of ro·ses to her grand·pa's grav*e*. Of c**ou**rse, C**ou**rtney m**ou**rn*e*d and wish*e*d for his s**ou**l to rest in peac*e*.

14

Chapter 2: Long ō - Courtney

 Copy these words and do not try to guess their spelling. Look at each word before you begin to copy it and do not look away from it until you are confident that you can spell it correctly. Don't let your hand alone do the copying; think actively about each word you are about to copy:

soul	sole	mould	mold
_____	_____	_____	_____
shoulder	course	coarse	four
_____	_____	_____	_____
for	your	pour	mourn
_____	_____	_____	_____
mourning	morning	dough	doe
_____	_____	_____	_____
your	yore	court	bourgeois
_____	_____	_____	_____
bourgeoisie	bouquet	dough	though
_____	_____	_____	_____
although	borough	thorough	Courtney
_____	_____	_____	_____
courthouse	courtyard	courtly	course
_____	_____	_____	_____
source	resource	resourceful	pour
_____	_____	_____	_____
pours	poured	pore	pores
_____	_____	_____	_____

1. Write five or more words that contain the long ō sound spelled with the "ōu" phonic. Example: soul

_____ _____ _____ _____ _____ _____

_____ _____ _____ _____ _____ _____

2. Write five or more sentences using words that contain the long ō spelled with "ōu." Example: Courtney went to the courthouse.

1. _____

2. _____

3. _____

4. _____

5. _____

6. _____

7. _____

8. _____

9. _____

10. _____

Chapter 3: The long ō sound spelled with "oe" as in "Joe"

The third way to spell the long ō sound is with the "oe" phonic as in "Joe."

Lesson 1: Meaning of a Long Vowel

> **Memorize:** The long "o" sounds like the name of the letter **O**.

The "o" is said to have a long sound when it sounds like the name of the letter **O**. The "o" as in "toe" sounds like the name of the letter **O** and that makes it a long ō.

The Homonyms' Theory in this case would be that perhaps this "oe" spelling pattern of long ō was first used to tell apart homonyms like "toe" and "tow," and once a new spelling pattern was used to tell apart any two words, more words ended up being spelled with it.

Compare these homonyms of long ō:

toe, tow	throe, throw	throes, throws
throne, thrown	roe, row	roes, rows, rose
sloe, slow	Moe, mow	floe, flow

17

Lesson 2: The two vowels walking Rule

Memorize: When two vowels are walking, the first one does the talking.

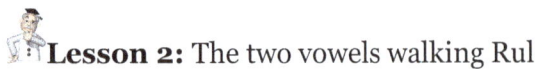 As in "J**oe**" when the two vowels "**o**" and "**e**" are next to each other (walking), the first one "**o**" does the talking and the second one "**e**" is silent.

The first one "**o**" does the talking means it has a sound and that sound is a long sound, just like the name of the letter **O**. The silent "**e**" is there just to help the "**o**" say **O**. When we say that the "**o**" does the talking, we mean the "**o**" is able to sound like the name of the letter **O**. Being able to say the name of the letter **O** means the "**o**" is long.

Similarly and as in the syllable "t**oe**d´" in "tip·t**oe**d´," when "**o**" and "**e**" are next to each other in a stressed syllable, the "**o**" has the sound of the letter **O**, and the "**e**" is silent.

toe or two

This "**oe**" spelling pattern of long **ō** is useful to tell apart homonyms like "t**oe**" and "t**ow**."

Know that the two vowels walking rule applies only to two vowels that are in the same syllable and that syllable must be stressed. Furthermore, the rule applies only to specific two vowels, not to any two vowels that are next to one another. All such specific two vowels are made available in this book.

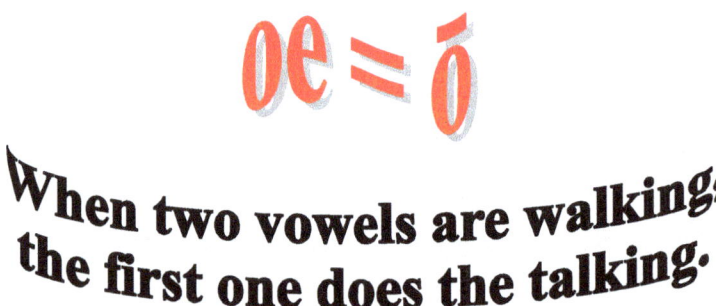

Lesson 3: The "oe" phonic occurs in approximately **24** words (11 one-syllable words)

| toe | Joe | Moe | foe | floe | sloe |
| roe | throe | doe | hoe | woe | |

toe · tip·toe · tip·toed
tip·toe·ing · Joe · Moe
foe · foes · floe
floes · woe · woes
throe · throes · roe
roes · doe · hoe
hoes · sloe · sloes
al·oe · o·boe · o·boes

Good Job!

Lesson 4: The "ōe" words in a story about "Joe"

Joe and Moe are not foes. Joe and Moe played the o·boe. Joe and Moe tip·toed when they walked in the woods near a frigh·tened doe. Joe and Moe picked up some sloe. Joe fed a small roe. Joe broke the soil with a hoe.

Joe fell on·to a floe and hurt his toe. Joe was in the throes of woe. Joe rubbed al·oe on his toe. Joe's foes took ad·van·tage of Joe, but Moe took care of Joe. Moe was learn·ing phon·ics and said,

"Joe ate a sloe. Mel·low was not slow."

"Joe hurt his toe. Mel·low called a tow truck to tow his car a·way."

"Joe is in the throes of pain. Mel·low throws a·way his lawn·mower."

Chapter 3: Long ō - Joe

 Copy these words and do not try to guess their spelling. Look at each word before you begin to copy it and do not look away from it until you know you can spell it. Imagine that your eyes are a camera; take a detailed picture of each word before you look away from it and before you begin to copy it:

toe	tiptoe	foe	floe
woe	roe	throe	doe
hoe	sloe	aloe	oboe
toe	tow	throe	throw
throes	throws	throne	thrown
roe	row	roes	rows
rose	sloe	slow	Moe
mow	mows	mowing	lawnmower
floe	flow	Joe	foe
foes	floe	woe	hoes
hose	sloes	slows	tiptoed

21

1. Write five or more words that contain the long ō spelled with the "ōe" phonic. Example: toe

_____   _____   _____   _____   _____   _____

_____   _____   _____   _____   _____   _____

2. Write five or more sentences using words that contain the long ō spelled with "ōe." Example: Joe hurt his toe.

1. _____

2. _____

3. _____

4. _____

5. _____

6. _____

7. _____

8. _____

9. _____

10. _____

Chapter 4: The long ō sound spelled with "oa" as in "Joan"

The fourth way to spell the long ō sound is with the "ōa" phonic as in "coat."

Lesson 1: Meaning of a Long Vowel

Memorize: The long "o" sounds like the name of the letter **O**.

Compare "cot" with "coat." The "o" is said to have a long sound when it sounds like the name of the letter **O**. The "o" as in "coat" sounds like the name of the letter **O** and that makes it a long ō. The "o" in "cot" does not sound like the name of the letter **O**. Without the silent "a," we would have "cot" not "coat." The "o" in "cot" has a unique short ŏ sound.

Furthermore, this "oa" phonic is useful to tell apart homonyms like roam and Rome, soar and sore, oar and or, board and bored, toad and towed, coarse and course, and hoarse and horse.

Compare short ŏ with long ō in these words:

got, goat　　　　　cot, coat　　　　　sock, soak

clock, cloak　　　　God, goad　　　　Todd, toad

rod, road　　　　　cost, coast　　　　John, Joan

Lesson 2: The two vowels walking Rule

Memorize: When two vowels are walking, the first one does the talking.

ōa...coat Compare "cot" with "coat." As in "coat," when the two vowels "o" and "a" are next to each other (walking), the first one "o" does the talking and the second one "a" is silent.

The first one "o" does the talking means it has a sound and that sound is a long sound, just like the name of the letter O. The silent "a" is there just to help the "o" say O. When we say that the "o" does the talking we mean the "o" is able to sound like the name of the letter O. Being able to say the name of the letter O means the "o" is long. Without the silent "a," we would have the word "cot" not "coat."

Similarly and as in the syllable "coal´" in "coal´·mine," when "o" and "a" are next to each other in a stressed syllable, the "o" has the long sound of the letter O, and the "u" is silent.

board or bored

This "oa" phonic is useful to tell apart homonyms like "board" and "bored."

Know that the two vowels walking rule applies only to two vowels that are in the same syllable and that syllable must be stressed. Moreover, the rule applies only to specific two vowels, not to any two vowels next to one another. All such specific two vowels are made available in this book.

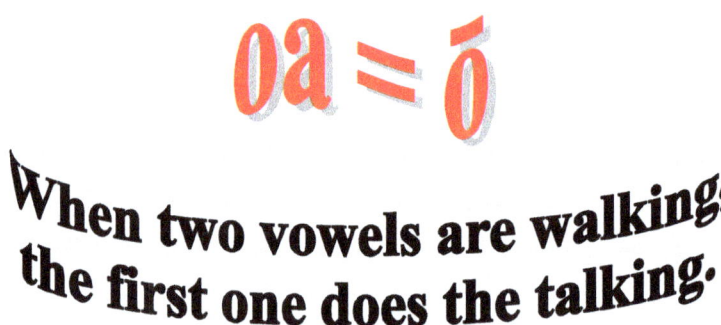

Lesson 3: The "oa" phonic in **144** words (48 one-syllable words)

Read aloud slowly together and in one rhythm:

coat	boat	goat	moat	throat	oat	float
gloat	bloat	oath	loath	load	toad	road
goad	poach	coach	roach	broach	toast	roast
coast	boast	moan	groan	loan	Joan	foam
roam	oar	coarse	hoarse	hoard	board	roar
soar	goal	coal	shoal	oak	soak	cloak
croak	coax	hoax	soap	oaf	loaf	

    coat   coats   coat·ed

    boat   boats   row·boat

    goat   goats   goat·ee

    moat   throat   oat

    oats   oat·meal   float

    floats   float·ed   float·ing

    gloat   gloats   gloat·ed

    gloat·ing   bloat   bloats

    bloat·ed   bloat·ing   oath

    loath   loathed   loath·some

    load   load·ed   load·ing

    up·load   up·load·ed   down·load

    down·load·ed   down·load·ing   toad

toads	road	roads
road·way	road·map	goad
poach	poached	coach
coach·es	coached	coach·ing
broach	broach·es	broached
broach·ing	roach	roach·es
cock·roach·es	en·croach	re·proach
re·proached	ap·proach	ap·proached
toast	toasts	toast·ed
toast·ing	roast	roasts
roast·ed	roast·ing	coast
coasts	boast	boasts
boast·ed	boast·ing	boast·er
moan	moaned	groan
groaned	loan	loans
loaned	loan·ing	Joan
foam	foams	roam
roams	roamed	roam·ing
oar	oars	coarse
coars·er	coars·est	hoarse

Chapter 4: Long ō - Joan

hoars·er	hoars·est	hoard
hoards	hoard·ed	hoard·ing
board	a·board	board·walk
chalk·board	black·board	board·ed
board·ing	roar	roars
roared	roar·ing	up·roar
soar	soared	soar·ing
goal	coal	coals
coal·mine	shoal	shoals
oaks	soak	soaks
soaked	soak·ing	cloak
croak	croak·y	croak·i·er
coax	coaxed	coax·ing
hoax	soap	soaps
oaf	loaf	loaves

Lesson 4: The "ōa" words in a story about "Joan"

Read aloud slowly whether reading in a classroom or alone:

Joan was from the East Coast. Joan's par·ents owned a coal·mining busi·ness. Joan's par·ents were load·ed with mon·ey. Joan's par·ents liked to hoard their wealth. Joan was not a boast·er and did not boast a·bout her family's wealth. Joan was a smart per·son; she was not an oaf. Joan's friend was a coach and he had a goat·ee. Joan's friend ate oat·meal, poached eggs, roast beef, toast from a fresh loaf of bread, and sipped on an ice-cream float. Joan's friend felt bloat·ed af·ter he ate. Joan did not gloat o·ver her friend's bloat·ing.

Joan felt cold and she had an ach·ing throat. Joan's coat was in her boat. Joan dropped her oar in the wa·ter. Joan's oar was made out of oak. Joan soaked her cloak in soap and wa·ter. Joan slipped on the soap's foam and fell. Joan roared with pain af·ter she fell. Joan's pain caused her to moan and groan. Joan couldn't go skate·boarding. Joan used to skate·board on the board·walk be·fore she fell.

Joan had a pet toad and a goat. Joan liked the moats she saw in some old mov·ies. Joan of·ten roamed a·round the town's roads to shop or to do noth·ing. Joan kept search·ing for fun ac·tiv·i·ties but was rare·ly ex·cit·ed a·bout any·thing, and her ap·proach wasn't work·ing for her.

Joan de·cid·ed to take fly·ing les·sons to keep her bus·y. Joan down·loaded some in·for·ma·tion a·bout fly·ing from the In·ter·net. Joan's goal was to learn a·bout fly·ing be·fore buy·ing an air·plane. Joan found out that the price of an air·plane fu·el was soar·ing high·er than ev·er.

Joan asked her friend who was a coach to give her fly·ing les·sons. Joan asked the coach to loan her his air·plane and he didn't. Joan didn't re·proach the coach, but she thought that he was a bit coarse when deal·ing with her. Joan de·cid·ed to quit be·ing the coach's friend and she broached the bad news to the coach. The coach was writ·ing his phonics' les·son on the chalk·board, and he got nerv·ous and stepped on a roach. The coach had writ·ten the fol·low·ing sen·ten·ces on the chalk·board:

"Joan watched the ea·gle soar. Rose had a sore throat."

"Did Joan have one oar in her boat, or did she have two?"

"Joan had a pet toad. Mel·low towed his car a·way."

"Joan's speech was neith·er coarse nor rude. Court·ney took a par·a·le·gal course."

"Joan's voice was neith·er hoarse nor rough. Rose had a horse?"

"Joan took an oath in court to say the truth."

"Joan's board of di·rec·tors stood on the board·walk, near the board·ers of Mexico, and bought a chalk·board. Mean·while, Rose was very bored as she wait·ed for them."

Learn to Spell 500 Words a Day by Camilia Sadik - O

 Copy slowly these words and do not try to guess their spelling. Look at each word before you begin to copy it and do not look away from it until you are 100% confident that you can spell it correctly:

coat	coated	boat	rowboat
goat	goatee	throat	float
oat	oatmeal	gloat	bloat
oath	loath	load	loaded
upload	download	toad	road
roadmap	goad	poach	coach
broach	broached	roaches	encroach
reproach	approach	toast	roast
coast	boast	moan	groan
loan	Joan	foam	roam
oar	coarse	hoarse	hoard

Chapter 4: Long ō - Joan

board	aboard	boardwalk	chalkboard
blackboard	boarded	boarding	roar
uproar	soar	soared	soaring
shoal	goal	coal	coalmine
oak	soak	cloak	croak
coax	hoax	soap	oaf
loaf	got, goat	cot, coat	sock, soak
clock, cloak	God, goad	Todd, toad	rod, road
cost, coast	toss, toast	John, Joan	bought, boat
ought, oat	groan, grown	roam, Rome	soar, sore
soars, source	shoal, shawl	coal, cool	coax, cokes
oaf, off			

1. Write 10 or more words that contain the long ō spelled with the "ōa" phonic. Examples: coat

_____ _____ _____ _____ _____ _____

_____ _____ _____ _____ _____ _____

2. Write 10 or more sentences using words that contain the long ō sound spelled with the "ōa" phonic. Example: Joan had a coach.

1. _____

2. _____

3. _____

4. _____

5. _____

6. _____

7. _____

8. _____

9. _____

10. _____

Chapter 5: The long ō sound spelled with "o-e" as in "Rose"

The fifth way to spell the long ō sound is with the "o-e" phonic as in "hope."

Lesson 1: Meaning of a Long Vowel

Remember: The long "o" sounds like the name of the letter O.

Compare "hop" with "hope." The "o" is said to have a long sound when it sounds like the name of the letter **O**. The "o" as in "hope" sounds like the name of the letter **O** and that makes it a long ō. The "o" in "hop" does sound like the name of the letter **O**. Without the final silent "e" in "hope," we would have "hop," not "hope." The "o" in "hop" has a unique short ŏ sound. Moreover, the "o-e" pattern is useful to tell apart two words like "sole" and "soul."

Compare short ŏ with long ō in these words:

not, note	dot, dote	rot, rote, wrote
cot, cote	cop, cope	mop, mope
lop, lope	pop, pope	slop, slope
hop, hope	hopped, hoped	hopping, hoping
rod, rode	nod, node	odd, ode
cod, code	mod, mode	nod, node
stock, stoke	jock, joke	sock, soak
wok, woke	rob, robe	glob, globe
bon, bone	con, cone	Tom, tome
com·ma, co·ma	Ross, Rose	pros, prose
Dos, dose	Sol, sole	doll, dole

Lesson 2: The "o-e" Rule

Rule: One consonant between two vowels is too weak to keep the two vowels from walking together.

hop or **hope**

ō-e...hope   Compare "hop" with "hope." We learned earlier as in "coat," that when two vowels are walking, the first one does the talking. This second rule in this chapter is built on that previous rule. As in "hope," one consonant between two vowels is too weak to keep the two vowels from helping each other (from walking together).

This means that when there is only one consonant between two vowels, like the one "p" in "hope," that one "p" cannot keep the two vowels "o" and "e" away from each other (from walking together). The two vowels in "hope" can still help each other and walk together in this way "o-e." The silent "e" can still help make the "o" long as if the two vowels were like this "oe" and as if the "p" were not between them. A dash in "o-e" represents not only the "p" but also any single consonant between the two vowels, like the one "t" in "note." Having only one consonant between two vowels is like having no consonant.

hŏpped or **hōped**

To prevent two vowels from helping each other, a consonant doubles as in hop, hopped, hopping, and this explains why we double the consonants after the short vowels. If you hear the sound of short ŏ, use "pp" after the "o" as in "hopped," and if you hear the sound of long ō, use one "p" after the "o" as in "hoped."

This same rule applies to other vowels. For instance, we use one "n" after the long "i" in "diner" and "nn" after the short "i" in "dinner." We use one "p" after the long "a" in "scraped" and "pp" after the short "a" in "scrapped." See these examples of any single consonant between two vowels being weak: fate, theme, dine, hope, cure

role and **roll**

Furthermore, this "o-e" spelling pattern is useful to tell apart two words like "role" and "roll."

> **Note** This "vowel-e" rule applies only to specific two vowels that fall in the same syllable, and that syllable must be stressed. All such specific vowels are presented in this book. See these examples of any single consonant being weak between two vowels: plane´, air·plane´, these´, Leb·a·nese´, side´, out·side´, scope´, mi´·cro·scope´, hope´, hope´·ful, fume´, per·fume´

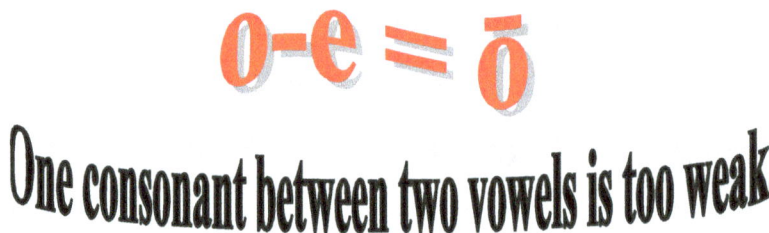

Lesson 3: The "o-e" phonic in 267 words (82 one-syllable words)

joke	woke	poke	broke	Coke	choke	smoke
stoke	stroke	yoke	hope	mope	rope	lope
slope	cope	scope	dope	pope	note	vote
wrote	rote	quote	cote	dote	code	ode
mode	node	robe	probe	globe	phone	tone
stone	cone	bone	prone	crone	drone	clone
lone	zone	Rhone	role	hole	whole	stole
sole	pole	bole	dole	mole	home	dome
tome	gnome	Rome	chrome	drove	grove	rove
cove	stove	clove	wove	hove	dove (v.)	nose
hose	chose	prose	rose	pose	close	clothes
hose	doze	froze	vogue			

joke	jokes	joked
jok·ing	jok·er	woke
a·woke	a·wok·en	poke
poked	pok·ing	pok·y
pok·er	broke	brok·en
brok·er	brok·er·age	Coke
choke	chokes	choked
chok·ing	chok·er	smoke
smokes	smoked	smok·ing
smok·er	stoke	stokes

stoked	stok·ing	stroke
strokes	yoke	yoked
pro·voke	pro·vokes	pro·voked
pro·vok·ing	in·voke	in·vokes
in·voked	e·voke	e·voked
hope	hopes	hoped
hop·ing	hope·ful	hope·less
mope	moped	mop·ing
rope	ropes	lope
lopes	loped	e·lope
e·lopes	e·loped	e·lop·ing
slope	cope	copes
coped	cop·ing	scope
mi·cro·scope	dope	pope
note	notes	noted
not·ing	no·ta·ble	no·tice
de·note	de·notes	de·not·ed
de·not·ing	vote	votes
vot·ed	vot·ing	de·vote
de·vot·ed	de·vot·ing	wrote
rote	quote	quotes
quot·ed	quot·ing	quo·ta·tion

Chapter 5: Long ō - Rose

cote	re·mote	pro·mote
pro·motes	pro·mot·ed	pro·mo·tion
de·mote	de·mot·ed	de·mo·ting
dote	dot·ed	an·ec·dote
code	en·code	en·cod·ed
en·cod·ing	de·code	de·cod·ed
de·cod·ing	ode	mode
ex·plode	ex·plod·ed	ep·i·sode
node	e·rode	e·rod·ed
robe	robes	probe
probes	probed	prob·ing
mi·crobe	mi·crobes	globe
phone	te·le·phone	phoned
tone	toned	ton·ing
stone	stones	lime·stone
corner·stone	cone	cones
bone	bones	hone
prone	crone	drone
clone	clones	cloned
clon·ing	lone	a·lone
lon·er	lone·some	lone·ly
lone·li·er	lone·li·est	post·pone
zone	o·zone	co·logne

co·lognes	hor·mone	hor·mones
cor·ti·sone	cor·ti·sones	Rhone
role	roles	role model
pa·role	pa·rol·ee	hole
whole	whole·some	stole
sto·len	sole	sole·ly
con·sole	ca·jole	ca·joled
con·dole	con·dol·en·ces	pole
poles	bole	dole
Dole	Cole·man	mole
home	dome	domes
tome	gnome	Rome
chro·mo·some	chro·mo·somes	chrome
drove	grove	groves
rove	roved	cove
cov·ert	stove	stoves
clove	cloves	wove
hove	dove (v.)	Beet·hov·en
nose	hose	panty·hose
chose	cho·sen	prose

Chapter 5: Long ō - Rose

rose	rose·mary	Rose
Rose·mar·ie	pose	posed
im·pose	im·posed	com·pose
com·posed	dis·pose	dis·posed
ex·pose	ex·posed	re·pose
re·posed	op·pose	op·posed
op·pos·ing	sup·pose	sup·posed
sup·posed·ly	trans·pose	trans·posed
jux·ta·pose	jux·ta·posed	en·close
en·closed	en·clos·ing	close
clothes	dose	over·dose
doses	lac·tose	glu·cose
doze	dozed	froze
fro·zen	vogue	brogue

Lesson 4: A list of **57** **r**-controlled words as in "St**ore**" (19 one-syllable words)

The "**r**" controls the sound of the vowel "o" in these words; technically, they are spelled like long ō but what should have been a long ō sound is distorted by the "**r**."

more	sore	tore	store	shore	chore	gore
core	score	snore	wore	swore	yore	pore
spore	fore	ore	lore	bore		

more	more·over	ig·nore
ig·nores	ig·nored	ig·nor·ing
sore	can·ker sore	sore throat
tore	store	stored
stor·ing	store·keeper	shore
sea·shore	a·shore	chore
chores	core	en·core
score	under·score	scored
snore	snored	wore
swore	gore	gored
yore	pore	pores
spore	fore	be·fore
pin·a·fore	fore·word	fore·stall
ore	lore	im·plore
im·plores	im·plored	im·plor·ing
de·plore	de·plored	ex·plore
ex·plor·er	ex·plor·ing	a·dore
a·dored	a·dor·a·ble	bore
bored	bor·ing	bore·dom

Lesson 5: The r-controlled words in a story about a "Storekeeper"

Storekeeper   The store·keeper ex·plored the i·de·a of o·pen·ing up a store near the sea·shore. The store·keeper's core be·lief was to think more be·fore act·ing. The store·keeper tore down an old worn out build·ing. The store·keeper scored big af·ter o·pen·ing up his new store.

The store·keeper was not bored. The store·keeper was not bor·ing. The store·keeper did not feel any bore·dom. The store·keeper's mind con·tained lore. More·over, the store·keeper a·dored his cus·tom·ers. The store·keeper wished to be an ex·plor·er.

The store·keeper had too many dai·ly chores. The store·keeper was torn bet·ween want·ing to trav·el and hav·ing to work. The store·keeper did not trav·el any·more. The store·keeper let a sigh and said, "Those were the days of yore."

The store·keeper had a sore throat but noth·ing could fore·stall the store·keeper's plans. The store·keeper dropped his ore in the wa·ter. The store·keeper did not ig·nore his ore. The store·keeper wore gog·gles and swore to find his ore. The store·keeper said that "sea·shore" is one words, not two.

Lesson 6: Spelled like long ō but not long ō, as in "glove"

Technically, the "o" in these **25** exceptions is spelled like a long **ō** but for various reasons it does not sound like long **ō**:

love	glove	dove (n.)
a·bove	shove	done
none	one	ones
gone	come	move
moved	prove	some
hand·some	whole·some	awe·some
lone·some	burden·some	tire·some
loath·some	grue·some	cumber·some

Remember that these words do not end with an "e":

bos·om	blos·som	ran·som

o·pos·sum

Copy all the above words and do not try to guess their spelling. Look at each word before you begin to copy it and do not look away from it until you are confident that you can spell it. Please use a separate sheet of paper to copy these words:

love	love	dove	above
shove	done	none	one
ones	once	gone	come
move	prove	some	handsome
wholesome	awesome	lonesome	tiresome
burdensome	loathsome	gruesome	cumbersome
bosom	blossom	ransom	opossum

Lesson 7: The "ō-e" words in a story about "Rose"

Rose chose her clothes carefully. Rose chose to close the door and try on some new clothes. Rose's clothes were always in vogue. Rose chose to buy an extra pair of panty-hose. Rose wore a nice cologne. Rose used a jump rope for her work-out. Rose chose to pose for an au·di·tion. Rose chose to en·close a cover letter with her ré·su·mé. Rose enclosed the cover letter. Rose was not a dope. Rose did not like to mope. Rose was able to cope with any problem. Rose eloped to get married.

Rose went to Rome and saw the pope. Rose loped around in Rome near the big dome. Rose brought souvenirs made of chrome from Rome. Rose bought a tome from Rome to bring home with her. Rose left Rome to return to her home sweet home. Rose read a fable about a gnome that lived in Rome. Rose enjoyed reading about chromosomes. Rose chose to recite poetry and prose.

Rose rose up early and drove around the orange grove. After that, Rose drove to the cove. Rose dove into the water at the cove. Rose used a rope and hove a rock at the cove. Rose came back home and listened to Beethoven's music. Rose made spaghetti sauce and froze it. Rose put three cloves of garlic in the sauce, put the sauce on the stove to simmer, and then sat down and wove a pair of mittens for her baby boy. Rose spoke on the phone with Rosemarie. Rosemarie, who is Rose's friend, chose to use rosemary in the cookie dough.

Rose did own her home and didn't owe any money on it. "Owning a home feels much bet·ter than ow·ing mon·ey," said Rose. Rose chose to buy a new wa·ter hose to wa·ter the back·yard. Rose could not smell the ro·ses be·cause her nose was plugged. Rose chose not to be nos·y when say·ing hel·lo to her neigh·bors.

Rose had many stands. Rose chose not to ex·pose her chil·dren to can·dy. Rose chose to op·pose smok·ing. Rose was op·posed to drunk·en driv·ing. Rose chose not to im·pose her choic·es on any·one. Rose chose to take the right dose of vi·ta·mins. Rose chose her dos·age af·ter read·ing the la·bels. Rose chose to dis·pose of her out·dated tab·lets. Rose chose not to stay in her old com·fort zone. Rose said, "Stay·ing in a com·for·ta·ble zone for a long time can cause a per·son to de·te·ri·o·rate." Rose wore her robe and sat down to think and con·tem·plate. Rose was con·cerned a·bout the fu·ture of our globe and the o·zone lay·er. Rose thought that it was a mir·a·cle to clone Dol·ly, the sheep. Rose was a well-read per·son, and she stud·ied the his·to·ry of human·kind since the Stone Age.

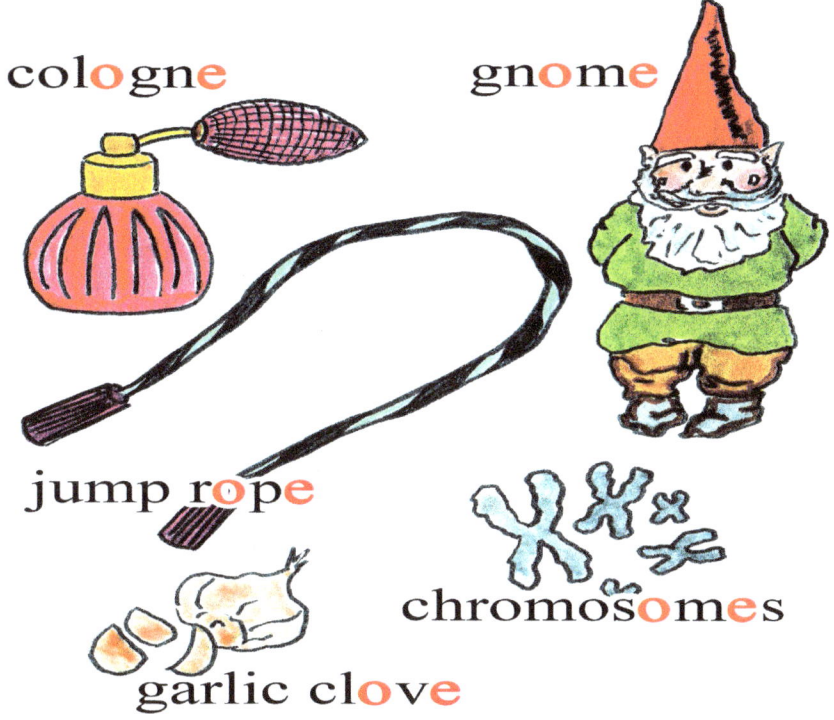

Rose was a suc·cess·ful an·thro·pol·o·gist and a sin·gle mom. Rose was of·ten a·lone but not lone·ly. Rose's ex-parents-in-law helped her with some of her chores. They came o·ver and used a hone to shar·pen all of her kitch·en knives. Rose was prone to post·pone her trip to Rhone, France. Rose had to have cor·ti·sone shot near her back·bone. Rose had to take hor·mone re·place·ments.

Rose's dad, Mr. Cole·man, was a lon·er. Mr. Cole·man was lone·some be·cause his wife had passed a·way. Mr. Cole·man had a soft tone of voice. Rose's whole fam·i·ly was hon·est. Mr. Cole·man dug a hole next to a tree bole and hid his val·u·a·ble coins in it. Rose nev·er stole any·thing from her dad. Mr. Cole·man used to be the sole o·wner of a shoe re·pair shop. Dur·ing the days of yore, shop o·wners like Mr. Cole·man were sole pro·pri·e·tors. Mr. Cole·man was an ar·ti·san who knew how to fit a sole on a shoe.

Rose played a good role in help·ing her fa·ther in his old age. Rose was a good role mod·el for her sis·ters and broth·ers as they were grow·ing up. All of Rose's sib·lings grew up to be good peo·ple.

Rose's fam·i·ly had some dif·fi·cul·ties dur·ing the time when her younger broth·er was in a ma·jor car ac·ci·dent. He was ar·rest·ed for drunk driv·ing af·ter his car hit a big pole and a cou·ple of pe·des·tri·ans. Her broth·er served his time and was la·ter let out on pa·role.

Hope

Hope is Rose's younger sis·ter. Hope was an at·tor·ney and an au·thor. Hope spoke pub·lic·ly a·bout the char·ac·ters in her book. One of the char·ac·ters' names was Mr. Dole, and Mr. Dole had had a stroke be·cause he used to smoke. Mr. Dole was a·bout to choke when he woke up one night. Mr. Dole's smok·ing was no joke. Mr. Dole used to be a suc·cess·ful brok·er that went broke. When he was young and be·fore his stroke, Mr. Dole used to play pok·er, watch TV late at night, and smoke. Play·ing pok·er pro·voked him to smoke more and more. More·over, Mr. Dole drank lots of Coke in·stead of wa·ter. Mr. Dole felt yoked to pok·er and smok·ing. Af·ter his stroke, Mr. Dole be·came pok·y and of·ten sat by his fire·place do·ing noth·ing but stok·ing and pok·ing the fire.

Mr. Dole learned that the core of the prob·lem that led to his stroke was the bad choi·ces he had made when he was young. Mean·while, he is al·so su·ing the to·bac·co com·pa·nies for pro·vok·ing him to smoke. Mr. Dole claims that their ads in·ten·tion·al·ly made smok·ing look cool, which pro·voked peo·ple to smoke. The court re·jec·ted Mr. Dole's case, but he swore he would in·voke the case. The court's rul·ing was not to ig·nore the fact that Mr. Dole made a free choice when he went in·to a store and bought his first pack of cig·a·rettes. Mr. Dole said, "I did not know then what I knows now."

When Mr. Dole was a young man, he was the type that did not like to hear an ad·vice from any·one—he thought that bad things could hap·pen to oth·er peo·ple but not to him. Mr. Dole had to ex·plore every·thing and dis·cov·er the an·swers the hard way. Mr. Dole didn't real·ize then that some of his bad choi·ces would be ir·rep·a·ra·ble.

Mr. Dole said that he was bored a lot when he was young. Mr. Dole said that those were days of yore. All that Mr. Dole could re·call was that out of bore·dom he ex·plored cig·a·rettes. He did re·mem·ber how his step·father used to snore and his snor·ing woke Mr. Dole up late at night. One night, Mr. Dole couldn't fall back a·sleep. He had fin·ished all of his chores and then he was bored. Mr. Dole wore his jack·et and head·ed to the store af·ter mid·night. Mr. Dole didn't know what to buy be·cause he wasn't hun·gry, so he bought a pack of cig·a·rettes.

Since then, Mr. Dole be·came ad·dict·ed to cig·a·rette smok·ing and he a·dored watch·ing TV late at night. Those TV com·mer·cials, Mr. Dole claims, made him be·lieve that smok·ing was a real cool thing to do. Sure e·nough, Mr. Dole didn't score an·y cool·ness from smok·ing; all he got was sore·ness that tore up his bod·y. Mr. Dole's bod·y felt as if it were poked by a bull's gore.

In her book entitled *The History of Cigarette Commercials*, Hope wrote a numerous analyses of all the commercials that were ever made throughout history to promote cigarette smoking. Critics said that her book contained lore. In the foreword, Hope dedicated her book to those suffering from secondhand smoke. Hope looked forward to seeing the foreword in her book being read by secondhand smokers.

Another character in Hope's book suffered from both smoking and secondhand smoking. Hope showed the pictures of this character in her book. The woman was in her mid thirties, but looked like she was one hundred years old. Her wrinkles were amazing. Doctors said that her pores were closed and blocked by smoke, and that air couldn't get through her pores. The woman who smoked had no idea that pores needed to breathe and that smoking and wrinkles were so closely related. She too, had to learn the hard way. Later on, the latter character spent lots of time sitting at the seashore hoping to heal her pores and to explore a new way of life.

Hope spoke about Mr. Dole's case before the judges. Hope said that Mr. Dole needed to appeal and to implore the judges to reconsider his case. Hope said that Mr. Dole didn't know and didn't have a special microscope to enable him to see what he was doing to his own body on the inside. Mr. Dole said that he hoped that someday someone would invent a special microscope for everyone to see inside of his or her own body. Only after his stroke did Mr. Dole have a clear idea of the scope of the damage done to his body.

Hope raised one major point against tobacco companies in her book. Hope spoke and said, "After legalizing the sales of tobacco, the tobacco companies should not have been al·lowed to ad·ver·tise; es·pe·cial·ly, not in such cru·el ways aimed di·rect·ly to·ward de·ceiv·ing the youth and the in·ex·pe·ri·enced."

At the end of her speech, Hope a·pol·o·gized and said, "My a·pol·o·gy if I am bor·ing you. I know that we are all used to hear·ing and see·ing sto·ries with hap·py end·ings, and that is how life ought to be, and it would be that way with·out smok·ing. How·ever, there aren't any sto·ries a·bout smok·ing that have hap·py end·ings. Smok·ing is no jok·ing mat·ter." Hope quot·ed her crit·ics when she spoke. Hope tried to pro·mote her book. Hope's lis·ten·ers cast their votes af·ter she spoke.

Sud·den·ly, Hope re·ceived a note from her re·mote cous·in who was look·ing for her and found her af·ter she spoke and he saw her on the news. Hope's re·mote cous·in used to write an·ec·dotes. Hope's re·mote cous·in dot·ed on her. Hope's re·mote cous·in was a very un·u·su·al per·son. A long time a·go, he showed Hope how to build a cote for her birds. He owed Hope an a·pol·o·gy for be·ing a·way. Ow·ing an a·pol·o·gy didn't mat·ter to Hope. Hope said, "No one owes me any·thing." Hope's cous·in wrote her an ode.

Hope became bus·y and had to hire an·oth·er sec·re·tar·y. Hope wasn't pre·pared for her sud·den fame, and she wasn't used to do·ing busi·ness in such a fast mode. Hope's tem·per was a·bout to ex·plode but she con·trolled her tem·per. Hope had to de·vote some time to show her new sec·re·tar·y the dif·fer·ence be·tween en·cod·ing and de·cod·ing and said, "To en·code is to con·vert plain lan·guage in·to codes. To de·code is to con·vert codes in·to plain lan·guage." Hope al·so showed her sec·re·tar·y the dif·fer·ent ways of spell·ing the long ō sounds and said,

"Rose sat on the king's throne. Mellow's sofa was thrown out."

"Rose was bored. Joan walked on the boardwalk."

"Rose was not alone. Joan had taken a loan from her bank."

"Rose is the sole owner of her company. Courtney prayed for his soul."

"Rose's leg was sore. Joan watched the prices soar."

"Rose's role was to be a role model. They will roll up their sleeves."

"Rose wore her new skirt. The war ended."

"Rose dug a hole, and her whole family watched her."

"Rose bumped her car into a pole. Paul is Paula's dad."

"No one stole Rose's car; its battery stalled."

Great Job!

 Copy slowly these words and do not try to guess their spelling. Look at each word before you begin to copy it and do not look away from it until you are certain that you can spell it correctly:

joke	woke	poke	broke
choke	smoke	stoke	stroke
yoke	provoke	invoke	evoke
hope	mope	rope	lope
elope	slope	cope	scope
dope	pope	note	denote
vote	devote	wrote	rote
quote	cote	mote	demote
remote	promote	dote	anecdote
code	decode	encode	ode
mode	explode	episode	node

erode	robe	microbe	probe
globe	phone	tone	stone
limestone	cornerstone	cone	bone
hone	prone	crone	drone
lone	alone	lonely	clone
zone	postpone	ozone	cologne
hormone	cortisone	role	parole
hole	whole	stole	sole
solely	console	cajole	condole
condolences	pole	bole	dole
mole	home	dome	tome
gnome	mole	chrome	drove

Learn to Spell 500 Words a Day by Camilia Sadik - O

🖎 Please use separate sheets of paper to copy the rest of these words:

grove	rove	cove	covert
stove, clove	wove, hove	dove, nose	hose, pantyhose
chose, prose	rose, pose	impose, compose	dispose, expose
repose, oppose	suppose	transpose	juxtapose, enclose
close, clothes	dose, lactose	glucose, doze, froze	vogue, brogue
lone, alone	more, moreover	tore, ignore	sore, soar
store, shore	chore, core	encore, score	snore, wore
swore, gore	pore, spore	fore, before	pinafore, foreword
forestall, ore	lore, implore	deplore, explore	adore, bore
yore, your	not, note	cot, cote, coat	rot, rote, wrote
dot, dote	cop, cope	mop, mope	lop, lope
slop, slope	pop, pope	hopping, hoping	hopped, hoped
hop, hope	rod, rode, road	nod, node	odd, ode
cod, code	mod, mode	nod, node	stock, stoke
jock, joke	sock, soak	wok, woke	rob, robe
glob, globe	bon, bone	con, cone	comma, coma
Tom, tome	Ross, Rose	pros, prose	Dos, dose
doll, dole	Sol, sole, soul	ore, or	fore, for, four
pore, pour	thrown, throne	bored, board	sore, soar
role, roll	sole, soul	wore, war	whole, hole
pole, Paul	stole, stall	coal, call	hole, haul, hall

Chapter 6: Long ō - Plato

Chapter 6: The long ō sound spelled with a stressed final "o´" as in "Pla·to´"

The sixth way to spell the long ō sound is with a stressed final "o´" as in "go´."

Plato, silo, sofa, mocha, cello

Lesson 1: Meaning of a Long Vowel

Remember: The long "o" sounds like the name of the letter **O**.

The "o" is said to have a long sound when it sounds like the name of the letter **O**. The "o" as in "o´·pen" sounds like the name of the letter **O** and that makes it a long ō.

Compare the different spelling patterns of long ō:
no´·ta·ble, no´, know   so´·cial, so´, sow

Lesson 2: The stressed final "o´" Rule

Rule: The stressed "o´" at the end of a syllable sounds like long ō.

no´ and **no´·ta·ble**

o´ = ō...o´·pen As in "o´·pen," the "o" sounds long when it falls at the end of a stressed syllable; it sounds like the name of the letter **O**, and that makes it a long **ō**.

The stressed final "o´" can be at the end the first syllable as in "o´·pen," at the end of the second syllable as in "com·mo´·tion," and at the end of a word as in "hel·lo´." In addition, the stressed final "o´" can be at the end of small, one-syllable words as in "no´." Compare the word "no´" with the syllable "no´" in "no´·ta·ble"; the "o" in both is at the end of a stressed syllable. This spelling pattern is the most common spelling pattern of long ō sound.

no´ or **know**

In addition, this pattern of long ō is useful to tell apart words like "no" and "know."

Not only the "o," but also any vowel that falls at the **end of a stresses syllable**, has a long sound of that vowel. Examples:

✓ The "e" in "me´·di·a" also falls at the end of a stressed syllable and it sounds long.

✓ The "i" in "bi´·ol·o·gy" falls at the end of a stressed syllable and it sounds long.

✓ The "o" in "po´·et" falls at the end of a stressed syllable and it sounds long.

✓ The "u" in "men·u´" falls at the end of a stressed syllable and it sounds long.

✓ The "a" in "ta´·ble" also falls at the end of a stressed syllable and it sounds long.

This rule teaches the spelling of long vowels in thousands of words and that is because the majority of long vowels occur at the end of a stressed syllable.

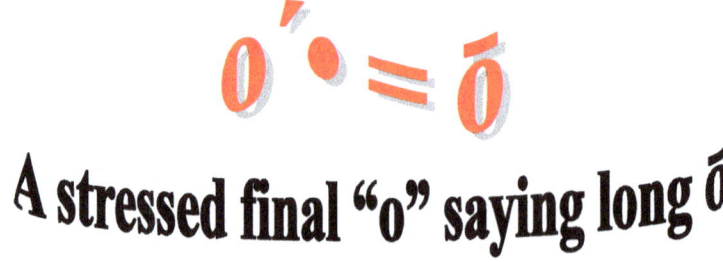

o´ = ō

A stressed final "o" saying long ō

Lesson 3: The "o ´" phonic in **133** words

Imagine there is a stress mark (´) on top of every final stressed "o" in these words:

o´·pen	o·pal	o·paque
o·pi·um	o·kay	o·kra
o·cean	o·bey	o·a·sis
o·ver	o·vert	o·vert·ly
o·va·ry	o·val	o·dor
hel·lo	cel·lo	po·lo
so·lo	ki·lo	si·lo
ze·ro	he·ro	her·o·ine
Cai·ro	bur·ro	in·tro
in·tro·duc·tion	quo	so
go	a·go	e·go
no	o·reg·a·no	in·fer·no
ca·si·no	pho·to	au·to
ve·to	in·cog·ni·to	bur·ri·to
ju·do	in·com·mu·ni·ca·do	in·nu·en·do
po·li·o	ech·o	dy·na·mo

pro·ba·tion	pro·cras·ti·nate	pro·cure
pro·claim	pro·fan·i·ty	pro·file
pro·gram	pro·hib·it	pro·long
pro·le·tar·i·at	pro·noun	pro·sa·ic
pro·tag·o·nist	pro·scribe	pro·té·gé

pro·to·col	pro·ton	po·tent
pro	pro·pri·e·tor	po·ny
po·em	po·et	po·et·ry
po·di·um	po·lar	op·po·nent
pho·ny	pho·bi·a	mo·lar
mo·cha	mo·tel	mo·tive
mo·tif	chro·mo·somes	mo·tion
mo·tions	com·mo·tion	no·tion
no·tice	no·ble	No·bel
do·nor	do·na·tion	so·cial
so·fa	so·lar	to·tal
to·ken	vo·cab·u·lar·y	vo·cal
rev·o·ca·ble	fro·zen	zo·di·ac
tro·phy	go·ing	co·her·ent
co·ex·ist	co·vert	yo·kel
ro·sa·ry	ker·o·sene	aer·o·bics
bro·chure	Cher·o·kee	bo·a
bo·gus	oh	ohm
so·lo	mo·dem	A·pol·lo
An·ge·lo	Spin·o·za	Ga·li·le·o
Ne·o·clas·si·cism	Co·per·ni·cus	Pla·to
Cho·pin	Mo·zart	Beet·ho·ven

58

Lesson 4: The final "o´" words in a story about "Plato"

Plato´ was named after a famous philosopher from ancient Greece. Plato took an intro course on ancient history. Plato went to Cairo. Plato stayed in a nice motel, sat on a sofa and drank café mocha. Plato saw the tomb of an ancient hero with his heroine wife. Plato took a photo with the cutest little burro in Cairo. Plato lived by an o´asis not far from the o´cean. Plato played water po´lo´. Plato liked judo.

Plato, as a solo, played the cello. Plato was also a poet and he wrote fine poetry. Plato went to the podium and read a poem. The motif of Plato's poem was about Chopin and piano. A noble person said, "You should be able to win the Nobel Prize for your poem." Plato's motive was not focused on winning a trophy. Plato was very vocal. Plato enjoyed hearing the echo of his own voice. Plato didn't enjoy prosaic as much as he did poetry. Plato's protagonists were Mozart and Beethoven.

Plato did not like anything phony. Plato said hello to that overt person over there. Plato bought a kilo of grain and stored in the silo. Plato always made sure that a medication was potent before he took it. Plato prolonged some of his work, but he was not a procrastinator. Plato believed that pronouns were just like nouns. Plato liked verbs more than nouns because verbs had motions. Plato used sophisticated vocabulary when he spoke.

Plato was an open-minded person. Plato didn't have a phobia from anything or anyone. Plato thought we could all coexist in a coherent manner and with·out fears. Pla·to's no·tion was that a cit·y pro·pri·e·tor and a yo·kel could co·ex·ist with·out any com·mo·tion. Pla·to was op·ti·mis·tic a·bout im·prov·ing the hu·man chro·mo·somes that would help us live in syn·chro·ni·za·tion.

Pla·to helped a pro·té·gé who was in in·com·mu·ni·ca·do for be·ing pro de·moc·ra·cy. That pro·té·gé had lived in·cog·ni·to. Pla·to learned a·bout him through an in·nu·en·do. Pla·to said the pro·té·gé was placed on pro·ba·tion. Pla·to wished for some·one to ve·to that de·ci·sion. Pla·to was pro·hib·it·ed from com·mu·ni·cat·ing with the pro·té·gé. Pla·to said the pro·té·gé was not a part of the pro·le·tar·i·at's move·ment. Pla·to did not wish for any·one to be pro·scribed. Pla·to o·beyed the law. Pla·to fol·lowed a spe·cif·ic pro·to·col when deal·ing with op·po·nents.

Pla·to was hand·some and looked like A·pol·lo. Pla·to re·ceived a bro·chure in the mail. Pla·to was go·ing to go to an aer·o·bic class six times a week. Pla·to no·ticed that his de·ci·sion was rev·o·ca·ble. Pla·to thought, "I need some of that time to read Spin·o·za's phi·los·o·phy and Dan·te's in·fer·no in·stead."

Chapter 6: Long ō - Plato

Copy slowly these words and do not try to guess their spelling. Look at each word before you begin to copy it and do not look away from it until you know that you can spell it correctly:

open	okay	odor	hello
hello	hero	zero	so
go	no	casino	inferno
veto	incognito	innuendo	echo
polio	dynamo	modem	potent
pony	poem	poet	prolong
procrastinate	profile	protocol	phobia
molar	mocha	motive	motif
notion	noble	donor	donation
sofa	social	motion	total
Plato	vocal	frozen	zodiac
trophy	coexist	coherent	going

yokel	rosary	kerosene	aerobics
_____	_____	_____	_____
brochure	Cherokee	solo	Apollo
_____	_____	_____	_____
oh	ohm	no	notable
_____	_____	_____	_____

Write 10 or more sentences using words that contain the stressed final "o´" phonic.

1. _____

2. _____

3. _____

4. _____

5. _____

6. _____

7. _____

8. _____

9. _____

10. _____

Chapter 7: The long ō sound spelled with "o + semivowel" as in "Soldier"

The seventh way to spell the long ō sound is with the "o + semivowel" as in "gold."

Lesson 1: Meaning of a Long Vowel

Remember: The long "o" sounds like the name of the letter O.

The "o" is said to have a long sound when it sounds like the name of the letter O. The "o" as in "cold" sounds like the name of the letter O and that makes it a long ō. The semivowel "l" is making the "o" long in "cold."

Compare the different spelling patterns of long ō:

poll, poleroll, roleboll, bole

Lesson 2: The ō + semivowel Rule

Semivowels can act like vowels and make the preceding "o" long.

ōm...comb The **l, m, n, r**, and **s** are semivowels, and they can sometimes act like vowels.

The semivowel "**l**" acts like a vowel here and makes the "**o**" long in "c**ol**d"; the semivowel "**m**" makes the "**o**" long in "c**om**b"; the semivowel "**n**" makes the "**o**" long in "**on**ly"; the semivowel "**r**" makes the "**o**" long in "tom**or**row"; and the semivowel "**s**" makes the "**o**" long in "m**os**t."

roll or role

In addition, this spelling pattern is useful to tell apart two words like "**roll**" and "**role**."

roll = rōll

The semivowel "l" makes the "o" long.

Chapter 7: Long ō - Soldier

Lesson 3: The "ō + semivowel" phonic in 49 words (30 one-syllable words)

old	cold	gold	fold	bold	mold	hold
told	sold	bolt	colt	jolt	volt	droll
scroll	stroll	poll	boll	toll	knoll	roll
yolk	folk	folks	most	host	post	ghost
gross	comb					

old	cold	gold
fold	bold	hold
mold	told	sold
sol·dier	bolt	colt
jolt	jolts	jolt·ed
volt	re·volt	droll
scroll	stroll	poll
boll	toll	knoll
roll	en·roll	con·trol
con·trolled	pro·to·col	swol·len
yolk	folk	folks
folk·lore	up·hol·ster·y	pol·ka
most	host	post
ghost	post·age	dos·age
host·ess	gross	as·bes·tos
comb	on·ly	to·mor·row
in·cor·ri·gi·ble		

Learn to Spell 500 Words a Day by Camilia Sadik - O

One of the semivowels follows the "o" in the following words. However, pronunciations of the "o" vary from one dialect to another. It is safer to consult your standard dictionary for the many ways that some of these words are pronounced:

lost	cost	host·age
fos·ter	boss	loss
toss	moss	os·trich
bomb	prom	some
come	re·solve	dis·solve
re·volve	in·volve	of·ten
of·fer	of·fice	cof·fee
off	scoff	scoffs

Copy slowly these words and do not try to guess their spelling. Look at each word before you begin to copy it and do not look away from it until you know that you can spell it correctly:

lost	cost	hostage	foster
boss	loss	toss	moss
ostrich	come	resolve	dissolve
revolve	involve	often	offer
office	coffee	off	scoff

Lesson 4: The "ō + semivowel" words in a story about a "Soldier"

The soldier was molded by the military. The soldier still folded his own clothes daily. When he went to war, the soldier had seen the windows jolt. The soldier rolled up his sleeves, sat down to eat eggs without the yolks, and then told us his life story. The soldier was funny and droll. The soldier was bold and daring. The soldier didn't have any hair to comb. The soldier was getting old. The soldier was cold.

The soldier used to have a barn and a colt. The soldier said that his folks owned a humble upholstery business. The soldier's folks grossed very little income. The soldier helped augment his folk's income most of the time. The soldier's dad had his hands swollen from sanding down old furniture. The soldier's only brother was ill from working in the asbestos factory. The soldier needed to live close to his folks. The soldier's folks didn't want him to travel anymore.

The soldier has had to put his own life on hold. The soldier wished to enroll in school again. The soldier sold his gold rings. The soldier felt trapped and wished to control his own destiny. The soldier didn't revolt or rebel; he said he only followed orders. At times, the soldier's situation seemed incorrigible. At other times, the soldier said, "Tomorrow will be a new day."

The soldier enjoyed the folklore he saw when he was in Poland. The soldier went to a house party and greeted the host and the hostess of that house. The soldier danced the polka with them. The soldier tied a bolt to their child's stroller. The soldier had to return to his post. The soldier sent his mail via a military post of·fice. The sol·dier did not have to pay for the post·age stamps. The sol·dier called home us·ing a toll free num·ber.

The sol·dier scrolled up-and-down the pag·es search·ing the en·gines to find his old friend. The sol·dier saw his old friend's pho·to on the In·ter·net, and thought he may have seen a ghost. Af·ter that, the sol·dier looked at the polls to see who was go·ing to vote for whom. The sol·dier said to him·self, "I vote for par·ties, not for in·di·vid·u·als."

Lesson 5: The "**or**" as in "b**or**n"

A pronunciation note: The l, m, n, r, and s are semivowels. As in these words, the vowel "o" is followed by a semivowel and its pronunciation can vary from one region to another.

Examples: The "**o**" in "**or**" may be pronounced like a schwa, or like a long **ō**, or like the "**au**" in "**au**ra."

Similarly, the "**o**" in "g**o**ne" may be pronounced like a short **ŏ** or like the "**au**" in "**au**ra." Some pronounce "**or**al" like "**au**ral."

It is best to consult your standard dictionary for the many choices of such pronunciations. To a person whose first language is not English, many such sounds followed by a semivowel sound like a long **ō**, and he or she often spells all of them with an "**o**."

As in "f**or**," the controlling "**r**" controls the sound of "**o**" and makes it have a special sound that is slightly different from the sound of long **ō**. Because the pronunciations of the "**or**" varies from one speaker to another and from one region to another, it is best to consult your standard dictionary for the many ways that the following words are pronounced.

Compare these words:

f**or**, f**or**e, f**our**   f**or**th, f**our**th   m**or**n, m**our**n

m**or**ning, m**our**ning   y**or**e, y**our**   p**or**e, p**our**

s**or**es, s**our**ce

Lesson 6: The "**or**" phonic in **85** words (21 one-syllable words)

or	born	horn	worn	morn	torn	thorn
corn	scorn	for	force	horse	torch	port
cord	corps	door	boor	floor	George	gorge

    or   **or**·der   **or**·deal

    or·di·nar·y   **or**·bit   **ō**·ches·tra

    or·chid   **or**·chard   **or**·gan·ic

    or·i·gin   **or**·gan   **or**·na·ment

    or·phan   **Or**·phe·us   **o**·ral

or·ange	born	horn
worn	morn	torn
thorn	corn	scorn
for·ty	for·mer	for·mal
for·tune	for·ward	for·ti·fy
for·eign	per·form	force
met·a·phor	ex·hort	hor·mone
ab·hor	horse	re·morse
Mor·gan	mort·gage	mor·al
mor·tal	morn·ing	Mor·ris
torch	tor·ment	tor·na·do
tor·ture	tor·tured	a·bort
as·sort	im·port	ex·port
air·port	re·port	re·sort
im·por·tant	port·a·ble	port·man·teau
ac·cord	dis·cord	re·cord
cor·ner	corner·stone	cor·dial·ly
cor·ti·sone	cor·po·ra·tion	in·cor·po·rate
cor·pus	corps	cor·ri·dor
or	door	Ec·ua·dor
en·dorse	floor	sub·or·di·nate
nor·mal	El·ea·nor	re·morse
met·a·mor·pho·sis	George	gorge
New York		

Chapter 7: Long ō - Soldier

Lesson 7: The "or" words in a story about "Eleanor"

Eleanor was born and raised in New York City. Eleanor's parents were foreigners; their origin was from Ecuador. Eleanor's father, Mr. Morgan passed away and her mother was a single mom. Eleanor's mother, Mrs. Morgan was forty-four and she took hormone replacements. Eleanor's two brothers were George and Morris. Eleanor's father had left them a fortune.

Eleanor was no ordinary person. Eleanor was easily fascinated by arts, by orbits, and by lots of other things. Eleanor read Greek mythology and discussed the metaphor in Orpheus with her brothers George and Morris. Eleanor said that Orpheus was a musician and a poet whose music had the power to charm wild beasts. Eleanor liked reading books like those of Franz Kafka's *Metamorphosis*.

George ran his late father's corporation and worked in imports and exports. George paid for the mortgage, and supported his family and his cousin who was an orphan. Morris was strong and felt fortified; he said he didn't feel forced to join the marine corps or the air force.

Eleanor was formal with her colleagues, but not with her friends and family. Eleanor wore formal clothes to work and many nice ornaments. Eleanor looked good walking by the door's corner going toward that corridor. Eleanor was genuine and she abhorred pretentious acts. Eleanor performed very well in her for·mer jobs. El·ea·nor played mu·sic in the city's or·ches·tra. El·ea·nor was a nor·mal young wom·an, and she had her own ups-and-downs. El·ea·nor was no fool and no boor.

One morn·ing, El·ea·nor asked her moth·er for a new pillow·case be·cause hers was worn out and torn. El·ea·nor gave her moth·er or·chids and ros·es for Moth·er's Day. El·ea·nor picked out the thorns from the ros·es and then gave them to her moth·er. El·ea·nor ate an or·gan·ic corn on a cob cul·ti·vat·ed from the near·by or·chard. She ate an or·ange picked from the or·ange grove. El·ea·nor ate as·sort·ed fla·vors of ice cream. El·ea·nor pre·ferred sit·ting on the floor. El·ea·nor scorned the dog for not lis·ten·ing. El·ea·nor wished she had a horse. El·ea·nor drove by an ice gorge. El·ea·nor liked to toot her new car's horn for at·ten·tion.

El·ea·nor was smart e·nough to know that she was not mor·tal. El·ea·nor signed a form to do·nate her or·gans af·ter her pass·ing a·way. El·ea·nor used to con·fuse the spell·ings of or·gans with or·i·gins, but she mem·o·rized the dif·fer·ence af·ter sign·ing that form. El·ea·nor for·ward·ed the form she filled out to those in charge of this or·deal. El·ea·nor wrote a short let·ter and en·closed it with the form; she signed the short let·ter with this phrase, "Cor·dial·ly yours, El·ea·nor Mor·gan." El·ea·nor tried to do the mor·al thing when·ever poss·i·ble. El·ea·nor didn't blame her·self and didn't have guilt or re·morse for mak·ing any mis·takes; she knew she was on·ly a hu·man.

El·ea·nor or·gan·ized her pri·or·i·ties and put im·por·tant things first. El·ea·nor en·joyed writ·ing and she brought her port·a·ble ta·ble and sat down to write a re·port a·bout some tor·ment·ed pe·ople, who were suf·fer·ing from tor·ture in their own home·land. El·ea·nor be·gan by re·cord·ing the facts. In her re·port, El·ea·nor in·cor·po·rat·ed the facts she re·cord·ed from ot·her e·vents. Ac·cord·ing to El·ea·nor's re·port, the dis·cord was be·tween a mi·nor·i·ty and a ma·jor·i·ty in that coun·try. El·ea·nor asked an eye·witness and his an·swers were the corner·stone for her re·port. The eye·witness saw cor·pus·es, peo·ple be·ing tor·tured, and death pen·al·ties be·ing or·dered. The mi·nor·ity was treat·ed as a sub·or·di·nate group of peo·ple and the lead·ers en·dorsed that. El·ea·nor's re·port was not o·ral; it was writ·ten. How·ever, it made a great deal of noise.

El·ea·nor took a short trip to that coun·try to see and hear for her·self. El·ea·nor went to the air·port with her port·man·teau. El·ea·nor spent some of her time in that coun·try's re·sorts; it was then when she de·cid·ed to be·come a free·lance jour·nal·ist. El·ea·nor wrote a·bout a count·less num·ber of oth·er is·sues a·fter that. More·over, El·ea·nor taught an ESL course as she was trav·el·ing; she wrote these sen·ten·ces on the board:

"Wal·ter was a bald·headed man. Don't be so bold and di·rect."

"Dawn wore a shawl. Joan saw the shoal."

"Scrawl me a note be·fore you scroll that mouse up-and-down."

"Joan lived in the West Coast and that didn't cost her much."

Learn to Spell 500 Words a Day by Camilia Sadik - O

Copy slowly these words and do not try to guess their spelling. Look at each word before you begin to copy it and do not look away from it until you know that you can spell it correctly:

metaphor	forward	foreword	form
perform	force	remorse	metamorphosis
hormone	abhor	Morgan	mortgage
mortal	moral	morale	more
Morris	remorse	torch	tormented
torture	tornado	gorge	George
nor	normal	Eleanor	Ecuador
corps	core	corpus	or, floor
subordinate	cord	accord	discord
door	corridor	endorse	corner
cornerstone	cordially	cortisone	corporation
incorporate	abort	exhort	assort

resort	port	airport	import
_____	_____	_____	_____
export	report	portable	potable
_____	_____	_____	_____
old	cold	gold	fold
_____	_____	_____	_____
bold	hold	mold	told
_____	_____	_____	_____
sold	scold	soldier	bolt
_____	_____	_____	_____
colt	jolt	volt	revolt
_____	_____	_____	_____
droll	scroll	scrolled	stroll
_____	_____	_____	_____
poll	boll	toll	knoll
_____	_____	_____	_____
roll	enroll	control	controlled
_____	_____	_____	_____
protocol	swollen	yolk	folk
_____	_____	_____	_____
folklore	upholstery	most	host
_____	_____	_____	_____
ghost	post	postage	dosage
_____	_____	_____	_____

host	hostess	gross	asbestos
comb	only	tomorrow	incorrigible
lost	cost	hostage	foster
boss	loss	toss	moss
ostrich	bomb	prom	some
come	resolve	dissolve	revolve
involve	often	offer	off
office	coffee	morning	mourning
morn	mourn	or, ore	worn, torn
forty, four	forty-four	forth, fourth	for, four, fore
for, foreign	origin, organ	horse, hoarse	sores, source
your, yore	York	pore, pour	oral, aural
cost, coast	bold, bald	shoal, shawl	scroll, scrawl

Chapter 8: The long ō sound spelled with "ōy" as in "Roy"

The eighth way to spell the long ō sound is with the "oy" phonic as in "boy."

**Lesson 1:** Meaning of a Long Vowel

Remember: The long "o" sounds like the name of the letter **O**.

The "o" is said to have a long sound when it sounds like the name of the letter **O**. The "o" in "boy" sounds like the name of the letter **O** and that makes it a long ō.

Notice that as in "boy," the "oy" phonic represents a unique sound of long ō.

Compare the "ōy" at the end of words with the "ōi" inside words:

boy, boil   toy, toil   soy, soil

coy, coil

Lesson 2: The "ōy" as in "boy" for the end of words

boy and boil

ōy...joy The "ōy" as in "boy" and the "ōi" as in "boil" have the same sound. Usually, the "oy" is used at the end of words, and the "oi" is used inside words.

However, persons' names are spelled with "oy," whether inside or at the end of words. For examples, the "oy" is in these persons' names: Roy, Troy, Joy, Joyce, Royce, Lloyd, Floyd, and McCoy.

The word "coyote´" is an exception to the rules.

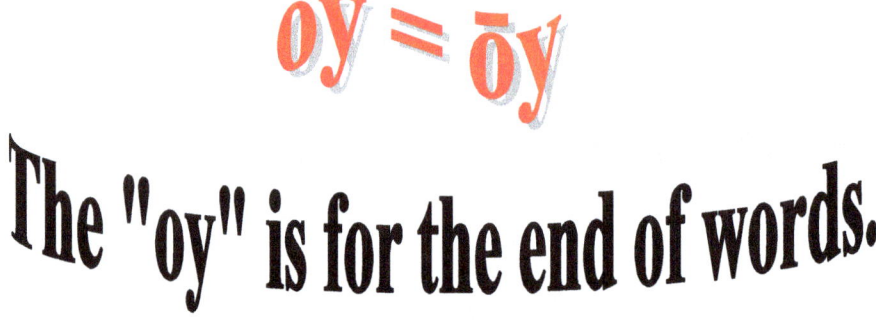

Lesson 3: The "ōy" phonic in 63 words (13 one-syllable words)

boy	toy	soy	coy	cloy	troy	Roy
joy	ploy	Joyce	Royce	Floyd	Lloyd	

boy	boy·ish	boy·hood
boy·friend	boy·cott	flam·boy·ant
toy	toys	toyed
toy·ing	soy	soy·beans
coy	coy·er	coy·est
cloy	cloyed	ploy
troy	Roy	joy
joy·ful	joy·ous	en·joy
en·joys	en·joyed	en·joy·ing
en·joy·a·ble	des·troy	des·troys
des·troyed	em·ploy	em·ploys
em·ployed	em·ploy·ing	em·ploy·ment
un·em·ploy·ment	em·ploy·er	em·ploy·ee
de·ploy	de·ploys	de·ployed
de·ploy·ment	al·loy	an·noy
an·noys	an·noyed	an·noy·ing
an·noy·ance	a·hoy	cor·du·roy
con·voy	con·voys	en·voy
en·voys	loy·al	loy·al·ty
roy·al	roy·al·ty	oys·ter

voy·age   foy·er   buoy·ant

McCoy   Troy   Joyce

Royce   Floyd   Lloyd

Lesson 4: The "oy" words in a story about "Roy"

Roy was from Troy. Roy had a boy·ish look. Roy was a coy boy dur·ing his boy·hood. There was no al·loy a·bout Roy. Roy was loy·al to his friends, Joyce, Joy, Troy, Lloyd, Floyd, Royce, and Mike McCoy. Roy en·joyed Joyce's com·pa·ny. Roy met Joyce in a foy·er when he went down·town to the un·employ·ment cen·ter. Roy said, "A·hoy" to greet Joyce. Roy was not Joyce's boy·friend.

Roy had a flam·boy·ant char·ac·ter. Roy wore cor·du·roy pants. Roy ate soy food and oys·ters, but he did not cloy. Roy drank soy·milk. Roy was not in the ma·rines and was not de·ployed any·where. How·ever, Roy knew a·bout the sea and nau·ti·cal i·tems. Roy had many big toys. Roy's toy was his big boat. His boat's buoy·an·cy made Roy hap·py. Roy went on a voy·age and met a roy·al fam·i·ly on the ship. Roy's ploy was not to an·noy the roy·al fam·i·ly in or·der to get em·ploy·ment with them.

Chapter 8: Long ō - Roy

Copy slowly these words and do not try to guess their spelling. Look at each word before you begin to copy it and do not look away from it until you are certain that you can spell it.

boy	boyish	boyhood	boycott
flamboyant	toy	soy	coy
cloy	ploy	troy	joy
enjoy	joyous	destroy	destroyer
employ	employment	employer	employee
deploy	deployment	alloy	annoy
annoying	annoyance	ahoy	corduroy
convoy	envoy	loyal	loyalty
royal	royalty	Joy	Joyce
roil	Roy	Royce	coil
coy	McCoy	Tory	Floyd
Lloyd	oyster	foyer	voyage

81

toil	soy	soil	coy
_____	_____	_____	_____
coil	royal	roil	royalty
_____	_____	_____	_____

Write 10 or more sentences using words that contain the long ō spelled with the "ōy" phonic.

1. _____
2. _____
3. _____
4. _____
5. _____
6. _____
7. _____
8. _____
9. _____
10. _____

Chapter 9: The long ō sound spelled with "ōi" as in "Detroit"

The ninth way to spell the long ō sound is with the "ōi" phonic as in "boil."

Lesson 1: Meaning of a Long Vowel

    Memorize: The long "o" sounds like the name of the letter **O**.

The "o" is said to have a long sound when it sounds like the name of the letter **O**. The "o" as in "b**oi**l" sounds like the name of the letter **O** and that makes it a long ō.

As in "bōil," the "ōi" phonic represents a unique sound of long ō.

Compare the "ōi" inside words with the "ōy" at the end of words:
b**oi**l, b**oy**   t**oi**l, t**oy**   s**oi**l, s**oy**

c**oi**l, c**oy**

Lesson 2: The "ōi" as in "bōil" for inside words

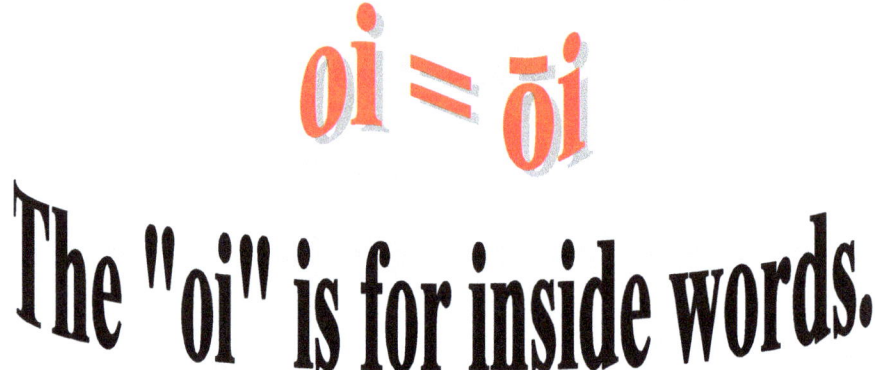

The "ōi" as in "bōil" and the "ōy" as in "bōy" have the same sound. Usually, the "ōi" is used inside words, and the "ōy" is used at the end of words.

oi = ōi

The "oi" is for inside words.

Lesson 3: The "ōi" phonic in 102 words (25 one-syllable words)

oil	boil	foil	toil	moil	coil	soil
spoil	roil	broil	coin	loin	join	joint
point	oink	moist	hoist	foist	void	voice
choice	noise	poise	coif			

oil	toil	toiled
coil	coils	coiled
soil	spoil	spoiled
boil	boiled	roil
broil	broil·er	em·broil
foil	tin·foil	doi·ly
moil	moiled	tur·moil
coin	coins	loin
join	joins	joined
join·ing	joint	dis·joint
point	points	ap·point
ap·point·ed	ap·point·ment	oint·ment
a·noint	poign·ant	oink
moist	mois·ture	mois·tur·ize
mois·tur·i·zer	hoist	hoist·ed
foist	foists	foist·ed

v**oi**d	v**oi**ds	v**oi**d·ed
a·v**oi**d	o·v**oi**d	de·v**oi**d
par·a·n**oi**d	par·a·n**oi**·a	em·br**oi**·der·y
fi·br**oi**d	Po·lar·**oi**d	as·ter·**oi**d
me·te·or·**oi**d	ste·r**oi**d	thy·r**oi**d
hyper·thyr**oi**d	hem·or·r**ho**id	hy·dr**oi**d
ty·ph**oi**d	hy·per·pl**oi**ds	cel·lu·l**oi**d
tab·l**oi**d	an·thro·p**oi**d	dis·c**oi**d

v**oi**ce	v**oi**·ces	v**oi**ced
v**oi**ce·less	ch**oi**ce	ch**oi**·ces
re·j**oi**ce	re·j**oi**ced	re·j**oi**c·ing
Il·li·n**oi**s	n**oi**se	n**oi**s·y
n**oi**·some	e·qui·p**oi**se	p**oi**se
p**oi**sed	p**oi**s·ing	p**oi**·son
p**oi**·son·ous	tur·qu**oi**se	b**oi**s·ter·ous

a·dr**oi**t	Det·r**oi**t	ex·pl**oi**t
ex·pl**oi**t·ed	l**oi**·ter	l**oi**·ter·ing
g**oi**·ter	f**oi**·ble	c**oi**f

Chapter 9: Long ō - Detroit

Lesson 4: The "ōi" words in a story about "Detroit"

Detroit The man from Det·roit had to toil and moil to find some oil un·der the soil. The man from Det·roit fixed the broil·er to boil eggs and to broil po·ta·toes. To keep his food from spoil·ing, he wrapped it with tin·foil. When he ran out of foil, he used a doi·ly to cov·er his food. The man from Det·roit went to Il·li·nois to search for oil wells. There was tur·moil in Il·li·nois and the man from Det·roit missed his ap·point·ment with those who ap·point·ed him to join the rest of the crew.

The man from Det·roit missed his fam·i·ly and used coins to call home. The wires and coils were cut off and he did not hear a voice or a noise. As a result, he loi·tered and lin·gered aim·less·ly. He saw a fly·ing sau·cer and was scared of the fly·ing dis·coid. He ex·pe·ri·enced some poign·ant anx·i·e·ty. He felt a void in his life. For a while, he was de·void of any wit.

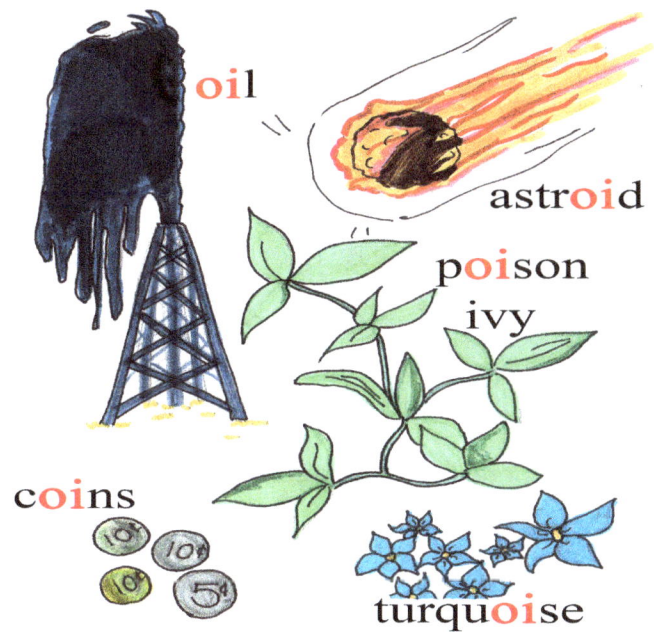

His choi·ces were lim·it·ed. The ground was moist and there was much mois·ture in the air. His joints were hurt·ing and he rubbed some oint·ment on them. As he loi·tered, he al·most got par·a·noid when he met a man with ty·phoid and a wom·an with a goi·ter. The wom·an's swol·len thy·roid gland was very vi·si·ble. He touched a tree and got poi·son i·vy. The man from Det·roit loi·tered un·til it be·came noi·some, at which point he had to a·void par·a·noi·a.

He stared at the me·te·or·oids and the as·ter·oids. Al·so, he took out his Po·la·roid cam·er·a and fo·cused on tak·ing pho·tos of pos·i·tive im·ages. He took a pic·ture of some tur·quoise flow·ers. He shot a pho·to of a wom·an do·ing em·broi·der·y. His next pho·to was of a wom·an a·noint·ing pe·ople dur·ing a re·lig·ious cer·e·mo·ny. He was un·a·ble to foist.

Sud·den·ly, the man from Det·roit met a group of bois·ter·ous ge·ol·o·gists hoist·ing their tools, and he re·joiced. They were put·ting on their tight coifs. Af·ter meet·ing the ge·ol·o·gists, he poised and gained some e·qui·poise. They were there to ex·plore the ar·e·a, but he was there to ex·ploit it. He had the choice to join them or to loi·ter and lin·ger a·gain. The man from Det·roit chose to stop loi·ter·ing and then he joined them.

Exceptions: The "**oi**" and the "**oy**" in these words sound like "**wi**":

choir	bour·geois	bour·geoi·sie
res·er·voir	rep·er·toire	Ren·oir
crois·sant	bu·oy	

Chapter 9: Long ō - Detroit

✍️ Copy these words and do not try to guess their spelling. Look at each word before you begin to copy it. Write slowly to avoid copying letters and words in a crisscross manner:

oil	toil	boil	coil
_____	_____	_____	_____
soil	spoil	roil	broil
_____	_____	_____	_____
embroil	foil	tinfoil	doily
_____	_____	_____	_____
moil	turmoil	coin	loin
_____	_____	_____	_____
join	joint	disjoint	point
_____	_____	_____	_____
appoint	ointment	anoint	poignant
_____	_____	_____	_____
oink	moist	moisture	hoist
_____	_____	_____	_____
foist	void	avoid	devoid
_____	_____	_____	_____
paranoid	paranoia	fibroid	asteroid
_____	_____	_____	_____
meteoroid	steroid	thyroid	hemorrhoid
_____	_____	_____	_____
embroidery	typhoid	tabloid	voice
_____	_____	_____	_____
choice	rejoice	Illinois	noise
_____	_____	_____	_____

poison	poisonous	poise	equipoise
turquoise	boisterous	Detroit	adroit
exploit	foible	loiter	goiter
croissant	bourgeois	bourgeoisie	repertoire
Renoir	reservoir	buoy	boil
boy	toil	toy	soil
soy	coil	coy	choir, quire

Write six or more sentences using words that contain the long ō spelled with the "ōi" phonic.

1. _____
2. _____
3. _____
4. _____
5. _____
6. _____

Section 2: Short ŏ

- The second sound of the vowel "o" is the short ŏ sound as in "Ron."

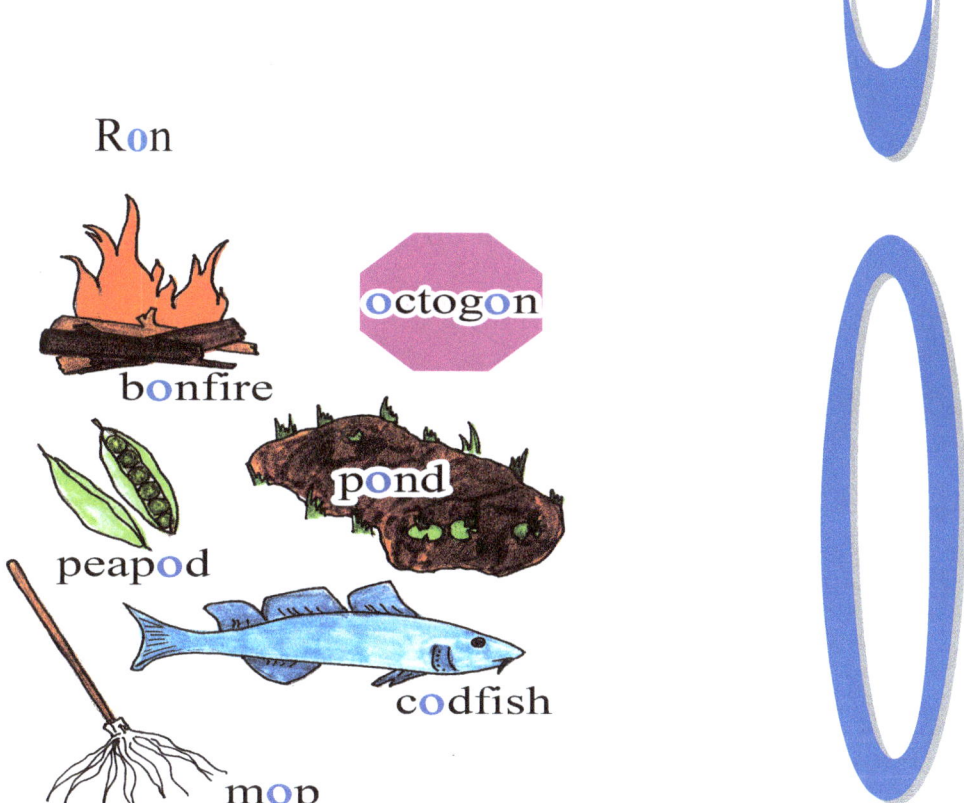

Chapter 10: The short ŏ sound as in "Ron"

Lesson 1: Meaning of a Short Vowel	**93**
Lesson 2: The short vowels' Rule	**94**
Lesson 3: The short ŏ phonic in **182** words	**95**
Lesson 4: The short ŏ words in a story about "R**o**n"	**99**
Lesson 5: Pronunciations of "o + semivowel" vary as in "l**on**g"	**100**
Lesson 6: Compare short ŏ with long ō	**101**
Homework	**103**

Chapter 10: The short ŏ sound as in "Ron"

10 ŏ...hot The short ŏ as in "hot" is the second sound of the vowel "o."

Lesson 1: Meaning of a Short Vowel

Memorize: Short "o" does not sounds like the name of the letter **O**.

The short ŏ is a unique sound that does not sound like the name of the letter **O**, and it is followed by one consonant (h**o**p) or two (h**o**pp**e**d). Compare the short ŏ in "h**o**p" with the long ō in "h**o**p**e**." The "**o**" in "h**o**p" has a unique short sound that does not sound like the name of the letter **O**. The "**o**" in "h**o**p**e**" sounds like the name of the letter **O** and that makes it a long ō.

Compare the short ŏ with the long ō in these words:

not, note	dot, dote	rot, rote, wrote
cot, cote	cop, cope	mop, mope
lop, lope	pop, pope	slop, slope
hop, hope	hopped, hoped	hopping, hoping
rod, rode	nod, node	odd, ode
cod, code	mod, mode	stock, stoke
jock, joke	sock, soak	wok, woke
rob, robe	glob, globe	bon, bone
con, cone	Tom, tome	com·ma, co·ma
Ross, Rose	pros, prose	Dos, dose
Sol, sole	doll, dole	

Lesson 2: The short vowels' Rule

Memorize: Consonants double after short "o," not after long "o."

As in "hop," the short ŏ does not sound like the name of the letter **O**. The short ŏ is followed by one consonant as in "hop" or two as in "hopped."

Compare "hopped" with "hoped." As in "hōped," we learned earlier that one consonant between two vowels is too weak to keep the vowels from helping each other (walking together) and that the first vowel does the talking. Therefore and as in "hŏpped," only two consonants "pp" can build a fence that is strong enough to keep "o" and "e" from helping each other.

hŏpped or hōped

Having only one "p" between "o" and "e," the "oe" can still help each other (walk together) and "hŏpped" would sound like "hōped." We need two consonants to follow a short vowel before adding "ed," "ing," "er," or "est" as in: hop→hopped→hopping→hopper. **When we keep the two vowels away from one another, we insure that the first vowel stays short and does not turn into a long vowel.**

The specific consonants that we double are **bb**, **dd**, **ff**, **gg**, **ll**, **mm**, **nn**, **pp**, **rr**, **ss**, **tt**, and **zz**; and we double them before adding endings that begin with a vowel like **e**d, **i**ng, **e**r, **e**st, **e**n, and **e**s.

Remembering that doubling the consonants is a process that needs plenty of practice; thus, it is important that you read the following words aloud; also, focus your vision on the doubled consonant after a short vowel.

Lesson 3: The short ŏ phonic in 182 words

Read aloud and focus on the two consonants that follow the short ŏ:

lot	slot	clot
plot	plot·ted	pot
pot·ter·y	Scott	Scot·tish
not	knot	knots
knot·ted	knot·ting	dot
hot	hot·ter	hot·test
jot	jot·ted	jot·ting
rot	rot·ted	rot·ting
rot·ten	shot	shots
got	be·got	be·got·ten
for·got	for·got·ten	bot·tle
mop	mopped	mop·ping
top	top·ping	hop
hopped	hop·ping	grass·hop·per
stop	stopped	stop·ping
shop	shopped	shop·ping
shop·per	chop	chopped
chop·ping	chop·per	plop
prop	pop	pop·u·lar
opt	op·por·tu·ni·ty	op·tion
op·er·a	op·er·a·tor	op·er·a·tion

God	God·dess	cod
nod	nod·ded	nod·ding
pod	pea·pod	sod
odd	od·der	od·dest
Todd	tod·dler	clod
Rod	Rod·ney	rod
jog	jogged	jog·ging
jog·ger	frog	dog
hog	bog	cog
cog·nate	sog·gy	smog
fog	fog·gi·er	egg·nog
log	logged	log·ging
clog	clogged	slog
flog	mon·o·logue	pro·logue
di·a·logue	ep·i·logue	prog·ress
rob	robbed	rob·bing
rob·ber	rob·ber·y	throb
throbbed	throb·bing	prob·lem
prob·a·ble	Rob	Bob
bob·by	job	cob
mob	knob	snob
snob·by	snob·bish	sob

sobbed	sob·bing	lob
blob	slob	hob
hob·nob	hob·by	hob·bies
wob·ble	ob·ject	ob·li·gate
ob·lit·er·ate	ob·nox·ious	ob·scene
ob·scure	ob·ser·va·tion	ob·sessed
ob·so·lete	ob·struct	ob·vi·ous
Oc·to·ber	oc·ta·gon	croc·o·dile
oc·cu·pa·tion	soc·cer	lock
locked	lock·ing	lock·er
rock	crock	stock
jock	dock	docked
shock	mock	mock·er·y
flock	knock	knocked
cock·roach	clock	mat·tock
sock	socks	sox
box	box·es	fox
fox·es	ox	ox·en
ox·y·gen	ox·i·dize	lox
pox	chicken·pox	prox·y
mom	mom·my	Tom
Tom·my	bomb	bombed
bomb·ing	bom·bard	bom·bard·ed

prom	prompt	im·promp·tu
prom·ise	prom·i·nence	pom·pom
om·nip·o·tent	com·ma	com
con	con·no·ta·tion	con·se·quen·ces
Ron	non	non·smok·er
bon	bon·fire	Don
pond	pon·der	ton·sil
ton·sil·li·tis	par·a·gon	on
lodge	lodg·ing	dodge

The prefixes ŏb-, ŏp-, ŏc-, ŏs, ŏm-, and ŏl-:

Note that consonant do not double after the prefixes "ob-," "op-," "oc-," "os-," "om-," and "ol-." They do not double because they are in a separate syllable plus they are usually followed by another consonant:

ob·ject	ob·sta·cle	ob·so·lete
ob·ser·va·tions	ob·vi·ous·ly	ob·li·ga·tions
op·er·ate	op·er·a	op·po·si·tion
op·po·site	op·por·tun·i·ty	oc·cu·pa·tion
oc·cu·py	oc·to·pus	oc·ta·gon
Oc·to·ber	Os·car	om·nip·o·tent
om·e·let	ol·ive	ol·i·gar·chy

Chapter 10: Short ŏ - Ron

Lesson 4: The short ŏ words in a story about "Ron"

Ron for·got to jot down notes be·fore he went gro·cer·y shop·ping. Ron turned on all the lights when·ev·er he felt de·pressed. Ron start·ed a bon·fire. Ron sat by the pond and talked with Don. Ron pon·dered a·bout the con·no·ta·tion be·hind a com·ment Don had made. Don didn't real·ize the con·se·quen·ces of his com·ment. Lat·er on, Ron real·ized that Don meant well. Ron said that Scott did not tie a knot with that Scot·tish girl. Don nod·ded a·gree·ing with Ron.

Soon af·ter that, Rod and Rod·ney came o·ver and brought some cod·fish with pea·pods. Don had hopped in·to the store, and stopped and shopped. Todd had a tod·dler ba·by boy and had to stay home. Rod came o·ver af·ter he fixed his cur·tain rods. Don thought it was odd that Todd wasn't there. Rod said that Todd had no op·tions ex·cept to stay home and mop the mess his tod·dler had made. Tom·my and Bob·by al·so joined the crowd. They were cook·ing chil·i in a crock-pot. All of them flocked a·round the fire. In the end, they went jog·ging and then they played soc·cer.

They dis·cussed the mean·ings of the words di·a·logue, mon·o·logue, pro·logue, and ep·i·logue. Bob hob·nobbed and did a good job ex·plain·ing the dif·fer·en·ces. Bob had lots of hob·bies. Bob was ob·sessed with read·ing. Bob didn't wob·ble or o·blit·er·ate when he spoke. Bob spoke a·bout ob·vi·ous things and said noth·ing ob·scure. For in·stance, Bob men·tioned that type·writers have be·come ob·so·lete and Bob also said that an oc·ta·gon had eight sides.

Lesson 5: The pronunciations of "o + semivowel" vary as in "l**o**ng"

Technically, the "**o**" in the following words is spelled like a short ŏ but its pronunciations vary from one speaker to another. The "**o**" is followed by a semivowel and it can sound like a short ŏ or like the "**au**" as in "t**au**ght":

on	w**on**	Am·a·z**on**
i·c**on**	p**on**d	l**on**g
be·l**on**g	pro·l**on**g	l**on**ged
p**on**g	p**on**e	g**on**e
s**on**g	s**on**gs	str**on**g
m**os**s	d**os**s	fl**os**s
t**os**s	f**os**·ter	fr**os**t
de·fr**os**t	pr**os**·pect	pr**os**·per
os·trich	b**os**s	b**os**s·es
d**o**ll	l**o**ll	kn**o**ll
j**ol**·ly	d**ol**·ly	tr**ol**·ley
v**ol**·ley·ball	H**ol**·ly	M**ol**·ly
p**ol**·len	p**ol**·ish	s**ol**·i·tud*e*
s**ol**·id	p**ol**·i·cy	p**ol**·i·tics
p**ol**·y·syl·la·ble	p**ol**·y·es·ter	**ol**·y·eth·yl·en*e*
p**ol**·y·graph	l·iv*e*	**o**·r**a**l
or·ang*e*	**or**·i·gin	to·m**or**·row
pr**of**·it	pr**oph**·et	pr**oph**·e·<u>sy</u> (v.)
pr**oph**·e·<u>cy</u> (n.)	pr**ov**·erb	

Lesson 6: Compare short ŏ with long ō

hop, hope	cot, coat	mop, mope
sop, soap	cop, cope	Rod, road
lop, lope	God, goad	pop, pope
Todd, toad	slop, slope	Ron, roan
not, note	John, Joan	rot, wrote
sock, soak	dot, dote	got, goat
rob, robe	glob, globe	sob, sober
non, known	cod, code	odd, ode
mod, mode	rod, rode	jock, joke
stock, stoke	wok, woke	stocked, stoked
bon, bone	Ross, rose	sod, sowed
con, cone		

Compare short ŏ with long ō in sentences and read aloud:

• Rose hoped her son would hop in her car.

• The cop was a·ble to cope with his prob·lems.

• He'll lop the tree branch, and then lope out of his door.

• He lis·tened to the pope while he was pop·ping some pop·corn.

• Don't mope a·bout the mess; mop your floor and feel bet·ter.

• He'll sop chips in the dip then he'll wash his hands with soap.

• Driv·ing on a slope road, he slipped on a slop of mud.

• He built a bon·fire and cooked a bone with his soup.

• I know the pros and cons of hav·ing an ice-cream cone.

• **None** of them worked for a non-profit or·gan·i·za·tion.

• Ron has a roan hoarse.

- **John** is mar·ried to **Joan**.
- He will **soak** his **sock** in wa·ter and soap.
- The **jock** wants to **joke** with us.
- I **stoked** the fire while I was sell·ing my **stocks**.
- I **woke** up and cooked veg·e·ta·bles in a Chi·nese **wok**.
- **Ross** brought me a red **rose**.
- He took off his **coat** and slept on a **cot**.
- He is **not** go·ing to write a **note**.
- The food did **rot** be·fore he **wrote** the note.
- He may **dote** be·fore he puts the fi·nal **dot** on his note.
- You will not **rob** my **robe** from me.
- She is **so·ber** and she doesn't **sob** any·more.
- It was **odd** that he wrote an **ode**.
- He ate some **cod** and wrote his zip **code** on the let·ter.
- Oh my **God**, I found a **goad**.
- **Rod** once **rode** in my car.
- **Rod** gave me a cur·tain **rod** and head·ed down the **road**.
- Which **mode** should we choose to de·sign a **mod** dress?
- They cov·ered my yard with **sod** and I **sowed** the seeds.
- **Todd** has a pet **toad**.
- Compare "grind, **ground**" with "**ground**" as in earth.
- Compare "wind, **wound**" with "winding, **rewind**."
- Compare **moll**, **mole**, **mall**, and **maul**.

Chapter 10: Short ŏ - Ron

Copy these words slowly in order to remember to double the consonants after the short vowel **ŏ**. Do not try to guess the spelling of a word; look at it before you begin to copy:

hot	hotter	hottest	forgot
forgotten	mop	mopped	mopping
hop	hopped	hopping	stop
stopped	stopping	shop	shopped
shopping	stopper	shopper	chopper
opportunity	god	goddess	nod
nodded	odd	odder	Todd
Toddler	jog	jogged	jogging
soggy	foggy	log	logged
logging	clogged	clogging	monologue
dialogue	progress	robbed	robbery
throb	Bobby	snob	snobbish

103

📎 Please use separate sheets of paper to copy the rest of these words:

not, note	dot, dote	rot, rote, wrote	cot, cote, coat
mop, mope	hop, hope	hopped, hoped	hopping, hoping
stock, stoke	comma, coma	Ross, Rose	pros, prose
cop, cope	lop, lope	pop, pope	slop, slope

rod, rode, road	nod, node	odd, ode	cod, code
mod, mode	jock, joke	sock, soak	wok, woke
rob, robe	glob, globe	sod, sowed	Tom, tome
Sol, sole, soul	doll, dole	sop, soap	god, goad
Todd, toad	Ron, roan	John, Joan	bon, bone
con, cone	non, known	got, goat	sock, soak

stock, stoke	stocked, stoked	object	obstacle
obsolete	observation	obligation	opposition
obviously	operate	operation	opera
opposite	opportunity	opportunities	occupation
omnipotent	Oscar	octagon	omelet

Section 3: Nine other sounds of O

■ The next **nine** sounds of "**o**" are minor sounds as in:
C**ow**boy, C**ou**nselor, Sn**oo**py, Ms. G**oo**de, **Ou**ght to, Wh**o**, L**ou**, Ren**o**ir, and D**ou**g

Chapter 11: The "ow" sound as in "Cowboy"

Lesson 1: The "**ow**" as in "c**ow**" for the end of words	107
Lesson 2: The "**ow**" phonic in **102** words	108
Lesson 3: The "**ow**" words in a story about a "C**ow**boy"	110
Homework	112

Chapter 12: The "ou" sound as in "Counselor"

Lesson 1: The "**ou**" as in "**ou**t" for inside words	113
Lesson 2: The "**ou**" phonic in **108** words	114
Lesson 3: The "**ou**" words in a story about a "C**ou**nselor"	116
Homework	118

Chapter 13: The "oo" sound as in "Snoopy"

Lesson 1: The "**oo**" as in "t**oo**"	119
Lesson 2: The "**oo**" phonic in **137** words	120
Lesson 3: The "**oo**" words in a story about "Sn**oo**py"	123
Homework	125

Chapter 14: The "oo" sound as in "Ms. Goode"

Lesson 1: The "**oo**" as in "g**oo**d"	127
Lesson 2: The "**oo**" phonic in **28** words	128
Lesson 3: The "**oo**" words in a story about "Ms. G**oo**de"	129
Homework	130

Chapter 15: Five minor sounds of "o": Ought, Who, Lou, Renoir, Doug

Lesson 1: The "**ou**" as in "**Ou**ght to"	132
Lesson 2: The one "**o**" as in "Wh**o**"	133
Lesson 3: The "**ou**" as in "L**ou**"	134
Lesson 4: The "**o**" says "**w**" as in "Ren**oir**"	135
Lesson 5: The silent "**o**" as in "D**o**ug"	136
Homework	137

Chapter 11: The "ow" as in "Cowboy"

The fourth sound of "o" is spelled with "**ow**" as in "c**ow**."

Lesson 1: The "**ow**" as in "c**ow**" is for the end of words

fowl or foul

As in "c**ow**," this "**ow**" phonic has a special sound that is different from the long ō sound in "snow." Perhaps this "**ow**" phonic as in "c**ow**" was used to tell apart two words like "f**ow**l" and "f**ou**l," and once the pattern was used to tell apart any two words, more words ended up being spelled with it.

In addition and because the "u" does not normally occur at the end of words, the "**ow**" as in "c**ow**" had to be used for the end of words, not the "ou."

Compare these words:

br**ow**s, br**ow**s*e*   c**ow**·er*ed*, c**ow**·ard   fl**ow**·er, fl**ou**r

f**ow**l, f**ou**l

107

Learn to Spell 500 Words a Day by Camilia Sadik - O

Lesson 2: The "**ow**" phonic in **102** words (26 one-syllable words)

n**ow**	c**ow**	v**ow**	w**ow**	pl**ow**	b**ow**	br**ow**s
br**ow**se	ch**ow**	D**ow**	**ow**l	h**ow**l	f**ow**l	c**ow**l
j**ow**l	gr**ow**l	pr**ow**l	cr**ow**d	cr**ow**n	cl**ow**n	dr**ow**n
fr**ow**n	d**ow**n	t**ow**n	br**ow**n	g**ow**n		

n**ow**	h**ow**	h**ow**·ever
c**ow**	c**ow**·boy	v**ow**
v**ow**s	v**ow**ed	v**ow**·ing
w**ow**	pl**ow**	pl**ow**ed
pl**ow**·ing	al·l**ow**	b**ow**
b**ow**s	b**ow**ed	b**ow**·ing
me·**ow**	br**ow**	br**ow**s
ey*e*·br**ow**	ey*e*·br**ow**s	br**ow**se
br**ow**sed	br**ow**s·es	br**ow**s·er
ch**ow**	ch**ow**s	D**ow**
en·d**ow**	en·d**ow**s	en·d**ow**ed
en·d**ow**·ment	k**ow**·t**ow**	p**ow**·er
p**ow**·er·ful	p**ow**·er·less	c**ow**·er
c**ow**·ers	c**ow**·ered	c**ow**·ard
fl**ow**·er	cau·li·fl**ow**·ers	p**ow**·der
ch**ow**·der	r**ow**·dy	r**ow**·di·er

108

Chapter 11: ow - Cowboy

row·di·est	how·dy	vow·el
vow·els	tow·el	tow·els
trow·el	Pow·el	owl
fowl	cowl	jowl
howl	howled	howl·ing
growl	growled	growl·ing
prowl	prowled	crowd
crowds	crowd·ed	crowd·ing
crown	crowns	crowned
crown·ing	clown	clowns
drown	drowns	drowned
drown·ing	frown	frowns
frowned	frown·ing	down
town	down·town	down·fall
down·hill	brown	gown
tow·er	tow·ers	bow·er
dow·er	dow·ry	show·er
show·ers	show·ered	show·er·ing

Lesson 3: The "ow" words in a story about a "Cowboy"

Cowboy The cow·boy bowed down tak·ing off his cow·boy hat, and said how·dy to all of us. The cow·boy asked, "How are you all do·ing folks?" The cow·boy was calm; he was not row·dy when he spoke. The cow·boy asked us, "How man·y cows do you have?" The cow·boy vowed to al·low us to use his plow. We said, "Wow!" to the cow·boy for al·low·ing us to use his plow.

The cow·boy comes here eve·ry now and then. The cow·boy had a smile·y face, and he nev·er frowned at us. The cow·boy's face was big and so was his jowl. The cow·boy had thick eye·brows. The cow·boy's eye·brows were raised when he saw us browse the In·ter·net. The cow·boy didn't shy a·way from us, nor did he cow·er. The cow·boy nev·er cow·ered, and he is no cow·ard ei·ther. The cow·boy is pow·er·ful; he is not pow·er·less. The cow·boy en·dowed a por·tion of his in·come to his un·ion.

cowboy hat

cow

owl

sunflowers

The cow·boy had sev·er·al cows and hor·ses. The cow·boy plowed his gar·den to plant var·i·ous types of flow·ers. The cow·boy plowed his back·yard to plant cau·li·flow·ers and sun·flow·ers. The cow·boy went to his bow·er to feed the fowls. On his way to the bow·er, the cow·boy said how·dy to a monk wear·ing a cowl. The cow·boy head·ed down·hill and heard an owl howl. The cow·boy's dog was growl·ing. The cow·boy's cat was me·ow·ing. The cow·boy finished his lit·tle prowl and came back home. The cow·boy took a quick show·er, and then left his tow·el to dry. The cow·boy read a book that con·tained all the chang·es in the way vow·els are spelled.

The cow·boy's wife was wear·ing a light brown night·gown. The cow·boy's wife changed and wore a dark brown gown. The cow·boy and his wife went to chow. The cow·boy had some clam chow·der soup and was full. The chow was crowd·ed and most of the crowd was his bod·ies. Mr. and Mrs. Powel were al·so at the chow. There was a nice crowd crowd·ing the place. The crowd watched tel·e·vi·sion and saw the new king be·ing crowned. Af·ter din·ing at the chow, the en·tire crowd went for a swim, and one of them near·ly drowned in the lake. How·ever, he was saved from drown·ing.

Af·ter swim·ming, the crowd went down·town near the big tow·er. They watched a clown ex·press·ing some signs a·bout the down·fall of civ·i·li·za·tion. The clown was from In·di·a, and he worked ver·y hard to save mon·ey for his daugh·ter's dow·ry. The clown had no wealth or dow·er. The clown kow·towed to so·lute the crowd.

Copy these words on separate sheets of paper. Don't let your hand alone do the copying; think actively about each word you are about to copy:

now	how	however	cow
cow	cowboy	vow	vows
vowed	vowing	wow	plow
plowed	plowing	allow	bow
bowing	meow	brow	brows
eyebrows	browse	browsed	browses
browser	chow	endow	endowed
endowment	kowtow	power	powerful
powerless	cower	cowers	cowered
coward	flower	cauliflowers	powder
chowder	rowdy	rowdier	rowdiest
howdy	vowel	towel	owl
fowl	cowl	jowl	howl
howled	howling	growl	growled
growling	prowl	prowled	crowd
crowds	crowded	crowding	crown
crowns	crowned	crowning	clown
drown	drowns	drowned	drowning
frown	frowns	frowned	frowning
down	town	downtown	downfall
downhill	brown	gown	tower
towers	bower	dower	dowry
shower	showers	showered	showering

Write **10** sentences using words that contain the "ow" phonic as in "cow."

Chapter 12: The "**ou**" as in "C**ou**nselor"

ou...out The fourth sound of "o" is spelled with "**ou**" as in "**ou**t."

Lesson 1: The "**ou**" as in "**ou**t" is for inside words

foul or fowl

ou...foul As in "f**ou**l," this "**ou**" pattern has the same special sound as the "**ow**" in "c**ow**." However, the "**ou**" occurs inside words, not at the end of words. The "u" in "ou" is no longer a vowel but it turns into the consonant "w."

Perhaps this "**ou**" phonic as in "f**ou**l" was used to tell apart two words like "f**ou**l" and "f**ow**l," and once the pattern was used to tell apart any two homonyms, more words ended up being spelled with it.

Compare these words:
f**ou**l, f**ow**l   fl**ou**r, fl**ow**·er   **ou**r, h**ou**r

113

Lesson 2: The "**ou**" phonic in **108** words (48 one-syllable words).

our	hour	flour	bough	plough	oust	ouch
couch	crouch	grouch	slouch	pouch	vouch	ounce
out	shout	scout	doubt	rout	lout	pout
clout	sprout	trout	drought	sound	ground	round
found	bound	mound	hound	wound	pound	count
fount	mount	loud	cloud	proud	mouse	house
spouse	blouse	foul	noun	south	mouth	

our	hour	ours
hours	hour·ly	flour
bough	plough	ploughed
oust	oust·ed	oust·er
ouch	couch	crouch
grouch	grouch·y	slouch
pouch	vouch	vouch·er
ounce	oun·ces	an·nounce
pro·nounce	re·nounce	de·nounce

out	out·standing	out·fit
out·look	out·doors	out·ing
out·source	out·age	shout
a·bout	scout	doubt
rout	lout	pout

114

Chapter 12: ou - Counselor

clout	clout·ed	trout
spr**ou**t	dr**ough**t	s**ou**nd
r**ou**nd	sur·r**ou**nd	sur·r**ou**nd·ed
a·r**ou**nd	back·gr**ou**nd	gr**ou**nd
f**ou**nd	pro·f**ou**nd	b**ou**nd
b**ou**nd·ed	b**ou**nd·ing	m**ou**nd
m**ou**nds	h**ou**nd	grey·h**ou**nd
w**ou**nd	p**ou**nd	pro·p**ou**nd
as·t**ou**nd	im·p**ou**nd	im·p**ou**nds
c**ou**nt	c**ou**nt·ed	dis·c**ou**nt
ac·c**ou**nt	ac·c**ou**nt·ed	ac·c**ou**nt·ing
c**ou**n·ty	b**ou**n·ty	f**ou**nt
f**ou**n·t*a*in	a·m**ou**nt	a·m**ou**nt·ed
a·m**ou**nt·ing	mount	m**ou**n·t*a*in
l**ou**d	l**ou**d·er	a·l**ou**d
cl**ou**d	pr**ou**d	h**ou**s*e*
m**ou**s*e*	sp**ou**s*e*	bl**ou**s*e*
r**ou**s*e*	a·r**ou**s*e*	tr**ou**·sers
l**ou**s·y	c**ou**n·cil	c**ou**n·sel
c**ou**n·sel*e*d	c**ou**n·sel·or	c**ou**n·sel·ing
f**ou**l	n**ou**n	pro·n**ou**n
s**ou**th	m**ou**th	de·v**ou**r

Lesson 3: The "ou" words in a story about a "Counselor"

The coun·sel·or has had an out·stand·ing rep·u·ta·tion. The coun·sel·or had an ex·cep·tion·al back·ground—he was well ground·ed in our com·mu·ni·ty. The coun·sel·or will coun·sel our city's coun·cil too. The coun·sel·or pro·nounced "coun·sel" and "coun·cil" in the same way.

The coun·sel·or had a u·nique out·look on life. The coun·sel·or wore a col·or·ful out·fit and his trou·sers were bag·gy. The coun·sel·or went out on Sat·ur·days. Last week, the coun·sel·or went out to din·ner and had fried trout bat·tered in flour with bean sprouts. There was a rout in town when he went out and lots of peo·ple were shout·ing a·bout the prob·lems re·sult·ed from the drought.

The coun·sel·or helped a grouch·y per·son treat his chil·dren bet·ter. The grouch·y per·son did not shout as much any·more. The grouch·y per·son learned to man·age his an·ger. For instance, he vent·ed out his an·ger while he ploughed and plant·ed flow·ers in his gar·den. He trimmed his tree branch·es and boughs. The grouch·y per·son nev·er said ouch when a thorn stung his hands—he en·joyed what he did.

The grouchy person was not a slouch anymore and he threw away his tobacco pouch. The grouchy person lost some weight and announced that he was going to count every ounce of the food he ate. The grouchy person sounded happier and he was now surrounded by people who loved him. The grouchy person was still the loudest one in the family. He still had many flaws, and this profound change in his life was bound to go away, if he did not continue to manage his anger—he found that out from the counselor.

The counselor helped a husband and a wife stay together. The husband and wife had some financial difficulties, but they loved each other. The counselor told them that there was hope as long as there was love. The couple's cars were impounded; they were living on welfare vouchers. They had to count every penny they spent, and they could only buy items from a discount store. Their bank accounts were empty—they were lousy in managing their lives. The spouses wounded up this way because of mismanagement. They were both held accountable for what had happened.

We took our son to the counselor and the counselor was ours for the next two hours. The counselor perceived that our son was about to turn into a potato couch. We have no doubt and we never doubted that this counselor would help our son. The counselor thought outdoor activities and outings were necessary to feel recharged with energy. The counselor did some outsourcing and found ways for the youth to be involved in outdoor activities. Our son improved profoundly and we were astounded. Our son shed pounds and wounded up reading aloud and memorizing phonics. I believe there are good counselors and bad counselors. Our community was proud of this counselor.

✍️ Copy these words on separate sheets of paper. Don't let your hand alone do the copying; think actively about each word you are about to copy:

our, hour	ours, hours	flour, flower	bough
plough	oust	ousted	ouch
couch	crouch	grouchy	slouch
pouch	vouch	voucher	ounce
announce	pronounce	renounce	denounce
devour	out	outfit	outstanding
outlook	outdoors	outing	outage
outsource	shout	about	doubt
scout	pout	lout	clout
rout	trout	sprout	drought
round	around	surround	ground
background	found	profound	bound
sound	mound	hound	wound
astound	pound	propound	impound
impounded	count	discount	account
mount	amount	mountain	fount
fountain	county	bounty	loud
aloud	cloud	proud	house
mouse	spouse	blouse	rouse
arouse	trousers	lousy	council
counsel	counselor	noun	pronoun
south	mouth	foul, fowl	flour, flower
our, hour			

✍️ Write **10** sentences using words that contain the "ou" phonic as in "county."

Chapter 13: The "oo" as in "Snoopy"

oo...boot The fifth sound of "o" is in "oo" as in "boot."

**Lesson 1:** The "oo" as in "too"

too, to, two

oo=ū...school The "oo" as in "too" sounds like a long ū. This "oo" pattern is useful to tell apart homonyms like "too, to, and two."

Except for the "ee" as in "meet," when two vowels double, they do not usually follow the rule that states that when two vowels are walking, the first one does the talking. The two vowels walking rule does not apply to **aa**, **ii**, **uu**, or **oo**. Instead, "oo" makes many special sounds other than the long ō sound.

Compare the "oo" pattern with other spelling patterns of long ū in these words:

too, to, two   shoo, shoe   shoot, chute

coo, coup   loon·y, lu·na·tic   loot, lute

Lesson 2: The "oo" phonic in 137 words (71 one-syllable words)

z**oo**	t**oo**	c**oo**	b**oo**	m**oo**	w**oo**	sh**oo**
b**oo**t	r**oo**t	h**oo**t	t**oo**t	l**oo**t	c**oo**t	sh**oo**t
c**oo**l	f**oo**l	p**oo**l	dr**oo**l	sp**oo**l	sch**oo**l	w**oo**l
t**oo**l	b**oo**m	d**oo**m	r**oo**m	br**oo**m	gr**oo**m	l**oo**m
z**oo**m	gl**oo**m	m**oo**n	n**oo**n	s**oo**n	sp**oo**n	c**oo**n
b**oo**n	l**oo**n	m**oo**se	n**oo**se	l**oo**se	b**oo**st	r**oo**st
ch**oo**se	b**oo**ze	**oo**ze	sn**oo**ze	c**oo**p	p**oo**p	l**oo**p
sn**oo**p	wh**oo**p	st**oo**p	dr**oo**p	tr**oo**p	s**oo**the	s**oo**th
sm**oo**th	b**oo**th	t**oo**th	h**oo**f	g**oo**f	r**oo**f	pr**oo**f
gr**oo**ve	f**oo**d	m**oo**d	br**oo**d	sp**oo**k	p**oo**r	m**oo**r
b**oo**r						

z**oo**	t**oo**	c**oo**
c**oo**ed	b**oo**	m**oo**
w**oo**	w**oo**ed	sh**oo**
sh**oo**ed	ta·b**oo**	tat·t**oo**
sham·p**oo**	sham·p**oo**ed	kan·ga·r**oo**
cuck·**oo**	ig·l**oo**	ig·l**oo**s
b**oo**ts	r**oo**t	r**oo**t·ed
h**oo**t	c**oo**t	l**oo**t
l**oo**t·ed	l**oo**t·ing	l**oo**t·ers

Chapter 13: oo - Snoopy

toot	toot·ing	shoot
cool	cool·ness	cool·er
cool·est	fool	fool·ish
pool	drool	drooled
spool	school	wool
tool	tools	hoo·li·gan
boom	boomed	doom
doomed	room	broom
groom	loom	zoom
zoomed	gloom	gloom·y
moon	noon	noon·time
bal·loon	spoon	spoons
soon	soon·er	coon
rac·coon	boon	ba·boon
ba·boons	loon	loon·y
moose	noose	loose
loos·en	loos·ened	boost
boosts	boost·ed	roost
roost·er	choose	choos·er
choos·y	booze	ooze
ooz·es	snooze	snoozed

Learn to Spell 500 Words a Day by Camilia Sadik - O

coop	poop	loop
loop·hole	snoop	snooped
whoop	Hula-Hoop	stoop
droop	drooped	troops
sooth	soothe	soothed
sooth·sayer	smooth	smoothed
smooth·er	smooth·en	booth
booths	tooth	tooth·ache
hoof	goof	goof·y
goof·ball	roof	proof
proofs	a·loof	groove
food	mood	mood·y
brood	doo·dle	spook
spook·y	boob	boo·by
poor	poor·er	moor
moors	boor	boors

Exceptions: blood, flood, floor

122

 **Lesson 3:** The "oo" words in a story about "Snoopy"

Snoopy

Snoop·y was a char·ac·ter in a car·toon. Snoop·y went to the zoo and saw a moose, a goose, a rac·coon, a ba·boon, a roost·er, a cuck·oo, a coot in a coop, a loon and a brood of birds in a coo, a bear liv·ing in an ig·loo, a kan·ga·roo, and many birds rest·ing in a roost. Snoop·y al·so saw butter·flies com·ing out of their co·coons. Snoop·y heard an owl hoot and a pi·geon coo.

Snoop·y was choos·y when choos·ing his friends. Snoop·y's best friends were moor, and some of them were fi·nan·cial·ly poor. None of his friends was boor. Snoop·y liked color·ful bal·loons. Snoop·y did not drink booze. Snoop·y want·ed a boost of en·er·gy. Snoop·y ate health·y food. Snoop·y didn't use a spoon to eat be·cause he was a dog. Snoop·y's mouth used to drool for a scoop of ice cream.

Snoop·y had a tooth·ache, and he need·ed a root ca·nal. Snoop·y had a loose tooth. Snoop·y doo·dled while he talked on the phone with his den·tist. Snoop·y's pain tab·lets were in a bag that drooped, and he could not reach the bag. Snoop·y need·ed those tab·lets to soothe out his pain. Snoop·y was doomed to have bad teeth. Snoop·y was in a bad mood. Snoop·y sham·pooed his hair. Snoop·y went for a walk when the flow·ers were bloom·ing, and when the weath·er wasn't gloom·y. Snoop·y's mood changed af·ter his walk.

Snoop·y sure·ly liked to snoop. Snoop·y had to toot the horns as soon as he saw what he thought was a troop of loot·ers try·ing to steal loots. Snoop·y drove off an·gri·ly and zoomed out of there quick·ly. Any·one could hear Snoop·y's car hoot. Snoop·y had no proof that those guys were loot·ers. Snoop·y real·ized his mis·take and thought that he act·ed like a goof·ball. Snoop·y was no stooge. Snoop·y was just tired and felt like a spoof. Snoop·y snoozed for the rest of that after·noon.

At night, Snoop·y watched the moon and went to bed ear·ly to go to school the next day. Af·ter school, Snoop·y swam in a cool swim·ming pool, and then he went out to shoot pool. Snoop·y used some tools to re·pair the stool next to the pool ta·ble. Snoop·y smoothed out the booth's sur·face un·til it be·came very smooth.

Snoop·y took off his boots and spent the rest of his after·noon fix·ing the roof of his class·room. There was ooz·ing mud and rain·water all o·ver the place. Snoop·y used a broom to sweep the room. Soon after that, Snoop·y wasted a spool of wool to make a thick loop to tie it a·round a hoop. Snoop·y loos·ened the loop and made a noose to cap·ture a horse by its hoofed foot.

Snoop·y met a groom. The groom was from the gen·er·a·tion of Ba·by Boom·ers. The groom used a broom to shoo the pi·geons, and Snoop·y said, "Boo!" to the groom. Ru·mors were that the groom had mooed and tried to woo his bride in·to mar·ry·ing him. The groom had a big tat·too, and hav·ing a tat·too was a ta·boo to Snoop·y. Snoop·y thought that the groom looked spook·y and some·what goof·y too. Snoop·y was no fool.

spoon
tooth
moon
tools
boots
broom

 Copy these words on separate sheet of paper. Don't let your hand alone do the copying; think actively about each word you are about to copy. Please use separate sheets of paper to copy:

zoo	too	woo	shoo
shoe	shoos	shoes	tattoo
taboo	shampoo	shampooed	kangaroo
cuckoo	boots	roots	looters
loot	lute	looted	looting
toot	shoot	cool	cooler
fool	foolish	pool	drool
spool	school	wool	tool
room	broom	groom	boom
doom	zoom	presume	gloom
gloomy	moon	noon	loon
lunar	loony	lunatic	moose
noose	lose	loose	loosen
booster	rooster	choose	choosy
sooth	soothe	shoo	chute
root	route	too	to
two	coo	coup	cope
doodle	dawdle	pool	pole

1. Write 10 or more words that contain the "oo" phonic as in "zoo." Example: boots

_____   _____   _____   _____   _____   _____

_____   _____   _____   _____   _____   _____

2. Write 10 or more sentences using words that contain the "oo" phonic as in "zoo." Example: We are close to the zoo.

1. _____

2. _____

3. _____

4. _____

5. _____

6. _____

7. _____

8. _____

9. _____

10. _____

Chapter 14: The "oo" as in "Ms. Goode"

The sixth sound of "o" is in "oo" as in "good."

Lesson 1: The "oo" as in "wood"

 This "oo" phonic is used to spell a specific sound of long **ū** as in "wood." The sound of "oo" as in "snoopy" changes to this special sound of "u" when it is followed by a "d" as in "wood" or by a "k" as in "book." Notice that this phonic occurs in root words that are one-syllable words.

wood or would

This spelling pattern is useful to tell apart homonyms like "wood" and "would." If a word contains a silent "l" as in "would," it is usually spelled with "ou," as in would, could, and should.

Compare the "oo" with "ou" in these homonyms:
wood, would

Learn to Spell 500 Words a Day by Camilia Sadik - O

Lesson 2: The "**oo**" phonic occurs in approximately **28** words (16 one-syllable words)

wood	good	stood	hood	book	took	look
shook	hook	rook	crook	brook	nook	cook
foot	soot					

wood	fire·wood	good
good·ness	stood	under·stood
hood	neighbor·hood	child·hood
book	took	look
looks	looked	out·look
shook	hook	rook
crook	brook	nook
cook	cooks	cook·book
Ms. Goode	foot	soot

Exceptions: bl**o**od, w**o**lf

Copy these words and do not try to guess their spelling. Look at each word before you begin to copy it and do not look away from it until you are 100% confident that you can spell it:

good, wood, stood   hood, neighborhood   look, took, book

_____   _____   _____

hook, shook, nook   rook, crook, brook   cook, cookbook

_____   _____   _____

wood, would   foot, soot   blood, wolf

_____   _____   _____

Lesson 3: The "oo" words in a story about "Ms. Goode"

Ms. Goode Ms. Goode was a very good per·son. Ms. Goode had a new out·look on life. Ms. Goode's good·ness was that she under·stood her needs. Ms. Goode had a nook for writ·ing. Ms. Goode wrote a book a·bout her child·hood. Ms. Goode's book shook up her neighbor·hood. Further·more, Ms. Goode took cook·ing les·sons. Ms. Goode looked for a good cook·book.

Ms. Goode wore her hood and stood by the fire·wood. Ms. Goode smelled the soot. Ms. Goode stepped on a hook and hurt her foot. Ms. Goode sat near a brook to feel bet·ter. Ms. Goode saw an old rook by the brook. Ms. Goode has had a hap·py child·hood. There were no crooks in Ms. Goode's neighbor·hood.

Write 10 or more words for each of the four sounds of "o" as in these examples:

cowboy	counselor	Snoopy	good
_____	_____	_____	_____
_____	_____	_____	_____
_____	_____	_____	_____
_____	_____	_____	_____
_____	_____	_____	_____
_____	_____	_____	_____
_____	_____	_____	_____
_____	_____	_____	_____
_____	_____	_____	_____
_____	_____	_____	_____
_____	_____	_____	_____
_____	_____	_____	_____
_____	_____	_____	_____
_____	_____	_____	_____
_____	_____	_____	_____
_____	_____	_____	_____

Chapter 15: Five minor sounds of "o": "Ought, Who, Lou, Renoir, Doug

Ought to, Who, Lou, Renoir, Doug

The following sounds of "o" are minor sounds because they occur in a very small number of words.

Ought to

"Ought to" is spelled with an "ou," not an "au."

Who

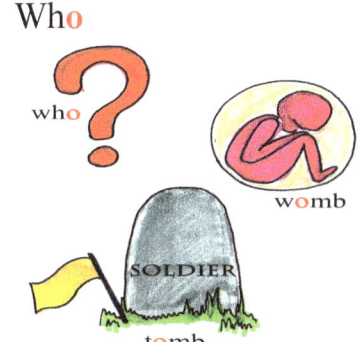

Lou

Renoir

Doug

131

Lesson 1: The "ou" as in "Ought"

ought or aught

The "ou" as in "ought" is a special sound, which sounds like the "au" in "aught." This "ou" pattern may have been created to tell apart two words like "ought" and "aught," and once the pattern was used, a few more words ended up being spelled with it.

In some dialects this sounds of "ou" is exactly like the short "o" sound, and "sought" and "sot" are pronounced alike, and "wrought" and "rot" are pronounced alike. This entails that creating this "ou" pattern was needed to spell two more homonyms, namely "sought and sot" and "wrought and rot."

Compare:
ought, aught   sought, sot   wrought, rot

The "ou" phonic in nine words

bought   brought   fought

sought   thought   thought·ful

ought   wrought   over·wrought

 Exceptions: "trough" is pronounced as "trouf"; sough is pronounced as "suf" or "sow"; and slough is pronounced as "slouf" or as "sloo."

He fought hard and thought that if he sought af·ter his son, bought him lots of books, and brought the books home, then his son ought to read them. How·ever, his son had not been over·wrought by any·thing. His son nev·er wrought.

To tell apart words like "ought" and "aught," remember these "au" words in this nonsensical sentence about Paul's daughter: Paul's daugh·ter caught the naugh·ty, haugh·ty, fraught, and dis·traught per·son and taught him to quit slaugh·ter·ing an·i·mals.

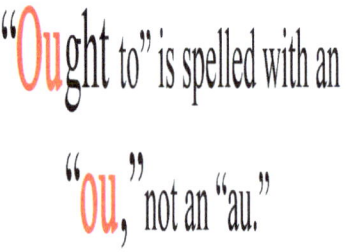

"Ought to" is spelled with an "ou," not an "au."

132

Lesson 2: One "o" as in "Who"

do or due

As in "do," the one "o" sounds like long **ū**. This spelling pattern is useful to tell apart words like "do" and "due" or "to, too, and two."

Compare the different spelling patterns of these homonyms:

| to, too | two, too | do, due |

The "o" as in "Who" occurs in approximately **nine** words:

to	in·to	do
who	who·ever	whom
whom·ever	womb	tomb

Who Who wants to do the home·work in class? The home·work is a·bout the "o" that sounds like a "u." Who·ever wants to go in·to the class·room may go now.

The teach·er said to mem·o·rize this sen·tence, "The ba·by was still in his moth·er's womb when she vis·it·ed the Unknown Soldier's tomb."

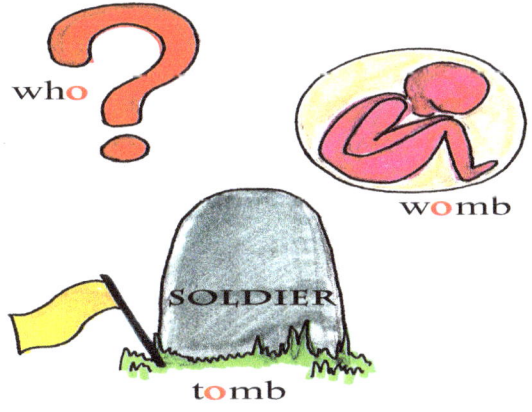

133

Lesson 3: The "ou" as in "Lou"

through or threw

The "**ou**" as in "y**ou**" sounds like a long **ū**. The "**o**" is actually silent in "y**ou**," and the "**u**" sounds long. This pattern is useful to tell apart homonyms like "thr**ou**gh" and "thr**ew**."

Compare the different spelling patterns of these homonyms:

thr**ou**gh, thr**ew**	L**ou**, l**ieu**	c**ou**p, c**oo**
tr**ou**pe, tr**oo**p	r**ou**te, r**oo**t	r**ou**tes, r**oo**ts

This "**ou**" phonic occurs in approximately **18** words:

Y**ou**	y**ou**th	thr**ou**gh
bor·**ou**gh	L**ou**	L**ou**·is
L**ou**ise	c**ou**p	c**ou**·pe
c**ou**·pon	s**ou**p	gr**ou**p
tr**ou**pe	r**ou**te	b**ou**l·e·vard
a·c**ou**s·tic	w**ou**nd	t**ou**r

Exceptions: c**ou**ld, w**ou**ld, sh**ou**ld

L**ou** lived in the bor·**ou**gh of Man·hat·tan. L**ou** went thr**ou**gh Broad·way B**ou**l·e·vard in or·der to get to work. L**ou** took a dif·fer·ent r**ou**te to a·void traf·fic. L**ou** rod*e* in a se·dan c**ou**·pe with L**ou**·is and L**ou**ise. L**ou** went out with a gr**ou**p of friends and they at*e* s**ou**p. L**ou** had a c**ou**·pon to pay for the s**ou**p.

L**ou** read a·bout the c**ou**p d'éta*t* in France. L**ou** used to t**ou**r in France with a sing·ing tr**ou**pe. L**ou** had learned a·bout a·c**ou**s·tics in school. L**ou** was a y**ou**th·ful type of a guy. Did y**ou** know that L**ou** was once w**ou**nd·ed in a war?

Chapter 15: Five minor sounds of O

Lesson 4: The "o" says "w" as in "Renoir"

ch**oir** or q**uir**e

As in "**o**ne," the "**o**" stops being a vowel, and it sound like the consonant "**w**." This spelling pattern is useful to tell apart homonyms like "ch**oir**" and "q**uire**."

Moreover and if we were to spell "**o**ne" with a "w" instead of an "o," we would end up with the word "**w**on." Most of the "**oi**" that sound like "**wi**" as in "Ren**oir**" are words derived from the French language.

Compare:
ch**o**ir, q**uir**e   **o**ne, **w**on

The "**o**" says "**w**" in approximately **13** words:

one	every·**o**ne	**o**nes
once	ch**o**ir	bour·ge**o**is
bour·ge**o**i·sie	res·er·v**o**ir	rep·er·t**o**ire
Ren·**o**ir	con·n**o**is·seur	cr**o**is·sant
bu·**o**y		

Renoir Ren·**o**ir was a fa·mous French paint·er. Ren·**o**ir may have had a cr**o**is·sant for break·fast. Ren·**o**ir may have lived near a res·er·v**o**ir. Ren·**o**ir may have passed by a bu·**o**y in the wa·ter. Ren·**o**ir may have heard the ch**o**ir sing at the rep·er·t**o**ire.

Once up·on a time, there was a class of pe**o**·ple in France called the bour·ge**o**i·sies—a bour·ge**o**is was an up·per mid·dle class per·son. The French rev·o·lu·tion in 1789 was lead by the poor a·gainst the bour·ge**o**i·sies and the ar·is·toc·rats. The **o**nes who were **o**nce in pris·on were re·leased af·ter the French rev·o·lu·tion on July 14, 1789.

135

Lesson 5: The silent "o" and the Homonyms' Theory

Doug or dug

Silent O As in "Doug," the "ou" sounds like a short ŭ because the "o" is silent. The silent "o" is useful to tell apart homonyms like "Doug" and "dug."

Compare:
Doug, dug   two, too

The silent "o" phonic is in approximately **19** words:

Doug	touch	dou·ble
cou·ple	cous·in	coun·try
jour·ney	jour·nal	ad·journ
cour·te·ous	peo·ple	sub·poe·na
Phoe·nix	coy·o·te´	soph·o·more
boul·e·vard	group	you
two		

Doug Doug was very cour·te·ous. Doug wrote for a couple of jour·nals. Doug has writ·ten a·bout hav·ing to dou·ble the con·so·nant af·ter a short vow·el. Doug wrote let·ters to a cou·ple of his cous·ins in Phoe·nix.

Phoenix

journal

coyote

Doug got in touch with two oth·er peo·ple from his group. Doug met with his group on Broad·way Boul·e·vard. Their meet·ing was ad·journed. On his way home, Doug stopped at the country·side and saw a coy·o·te. Do you know that Doug was served with a sub·poe·na right after he got home? Doug was dis·ap·point·ed and de·cid·ed to go on a jour·ney to be in a dif·fer·ent coun·try.

Chapter 15: Five minor sounds of O

Copy these words and do not try to guess their spelling. Look at each word before you begin to copy it and do not look away from it until you know you can spell it:

ought to	aught	sought	sot
wrought	rot	bought	brought
fought	sought	thought	thoughtful
overwrought	to	too	two
do	due	who	whoever
whom	whomever	womb	tomb
through	threw	Lou	Lieu
coupe	coup	coo	troupe
troop	route	root	routes
roots	you	youth	through
threw	throughout	borough	Louis
Louise	coupe	coupon	group

Learn to Spell 500 Words a Day by Camilia Sadik - O

boulevard	acoustic	wound	wounded
tour	choir	quire	one
won	everyone	ones	once
Renoir	reservoir	bourgeois	bourgeoisie
repertoire	croissant	buoy	Doug
dug	touch	double	couple
cousin	country	journey	journal
adjourn	courteous	people	subpoena
Phoenix	coyote´	sophomore	soup

Write five or more words that contain the minor sounds of "o" as in these examples:

bought	do	who	people
_____	_____	_____	_____
_____	_____	_____	_____
_____	_____	_____	_____
_____	_____	_____	_____
_____	_____	_____	_____

Section 4: Schwa of O

The twelfth sound of "o" is a weak sound called a schwa sound.

A schwa is a weak sound of any vowel.

- The schwa sound of "a" is as in "perm**a**nent."
- The schwa sound of "e" is as in "po**e**t."
- The schwa sound of "i" is as in "cred**i**ble."
- The schwa sound of "o" is as in "mem**o**ry."
- The schwa sound of "u" is as in "vir**u**s."

Chapter 20: The schwa sounds of "o" as in "Professor"

Lesson 1: Meaning of a Schwa ə	**141**
Lesson 2: The schwa sound of "o" in **70** words	**142**
Lesson 3: Schwa ə of "o" in a story about a "Profess**o**r"	**143**
Homework	**144**

Chapter 16: The schwa sound of "o" as in "Professor"

The twelfth sound of "o" as in "ru´·mor" is a weak sound called a schwa.

Lesson 1: Meaning of a Schwa

Memorize: The schwa is a weak sound of any vowel.

Why is it weak? The schwa is a weak sound because it falls in a syllable, which is not stressed. Also, most schwas are followed by a semivowel, especially by the semivowel "r" as in "mem´·o·ry´."

mem´·o·ry

Schwa ə As in "mem´·o·ry," this weak unstressed sound of "o" is called a "schwa" and its symbol looks like an upside-down "e" ə. Notice that other syllables in "mem´·o·ry" are stressed, but not the one where the schwa sound of "o" is.

Because the schwa of "o" has a weak sound, it is sometimes confused with the short ŏ sound, or with other vowel sounds like the "e" or "a." Most schwas of "o" are at the end of words.

A schwa is a name given to any weak "unstressed" or "barely heard" sound of a vowel. The vaguely heard sound of "o" can be confused with any other vowel sound. It is this weak and confusing sound of a vowel, which is called a schwa sound. You will better learn the schwa after studying all of the five vowels and comparing them.

Compare the schwa sound in "o" with other vowel sounds in these words:

tai·l**o**r, trail·**e**r   doc·t**o**r, car·pen·t**e**r   col·**o**r, cull·**e**r

do´·n**o**r, do´·**e**r   **o**p·pose, **a**·pol·o·gy   auth·**o**r, oth·**e**r

mem´·**o**·ry, sec·re·t**a**r·y

Learn to Spell 500 Words a Day by Camilia Sadik - O

Lesson 2: The schwa sound of "o" in 70 words

Notice that the weak sound of "o" is in a syllable that is unstressed:

im´·p**o**·tent	om´·ni·p**o**·tent	im´·pris·**o**n
e·quiv·**o**·cal	**o**·bit´·u·a·ry	**o**b·nox´·ious
ob·vi´·ous	**o**·blit´·er·ate´	**o**b·ses´·sion
ob·tain´	**o**·blig*e*	**o**c·cur´
of·fend´	**o**·pin´·ion	**o**·pos´·sum
op·po´·nent	**o**p·pos*e*	**o**p·press´
p**o**·di´·a·trist	p**o**·lic*e*´	p**o**·lit*e*´
p**o**l·lut*e*´	phi·los´·**o**·phy´	pr**o**·mot*e*´
pr**o**·mo´·tion	pr**o**·nun·ci·a´·tion	pr**o**·pel´
pr**o**·po´·nent	pr**o**·po´·sal	pr**o**·test´
cor´·p**o**r·a·tion	t**o**·ma´·to	t**o**·mor·row´
id´·i·**o**t	s**o**·lic·it´	mel´·**o**·dy
mem´·**o**·ry	mem´·**o**·ra·ble	su·pe´·ri·**o**r
in´·fe´·ri·**o**r	in´·te´·ri·**o**r	ex´·te´·ri·**o**r
er´·r**o**r	ter´·r**o**r	har´·b**o**r
la´·b**o**r	hu´·m**o**r	ru´·m**o**r
mi´·n**o**r	gov´·er·n**o**r	do´·n**o**r
ven´·d**o**r	splen´·d**o**r	ra´·z**o**r
cur·s**o**r	fa·v**o**r	ma·j**o**r
au·th**o**r	ad·vis´·**o**r/adviser	coun·sel´·**o**r
chan´·cel·l**o**r	coun·cil´·**o**r	in´·spect´·**o**r
doc´·t**o**r	pro·fes´·s**o**r	ed·u´·ca´·t**o**r
e·qua´·t**o**r	e´·quiv·**o**·cal	el·**o**·quent

Lesson 3: The schwa of "o" words in a story about a "Professor"

Professor The pro·fes·sor's Ph.D. was in Greek phi·los·o·phy. The pro·fes·sor had writ·ten a ma·jor cri·tique on Zeus, the om·ni·po·tent Greek God. The pro·fes·sor was a splen·dor au·thor. There was a ru·mor the pro·fes·sor was to be the next chan·cel·lor of his u·ni·ver·si·ty.

The gov·er·nor asked the pro·fes·sor to work di·rect·ly un·der him, but the pro·fes·sor de·clined po·lite·ly and pro·fes·sion·al·ly. He said he fa·vored lec·tur·ing phi·los·o·phy. The pro·fes·sor felt his role as an ed·u·ca·tor was much more wor·thy. The pro·fes·sor pro·mot·ed ed·u·ca·tion be·cause he be·lieved most so·cial and po·lit·i·cal cri·ses can be solved through ed·u·ca·tion. He said, "An ed·u·ca·tor is the big·gest con·trib·u·tor to so·ci·e·ty."

The u·ni·ver·si·ty chan·cel·lor, the city coun·cil·or, the stu·dent coun·sel·or, the ad·vis·or, the in·spect·or, and the doc·tor, all a·greed that the pro·fes·sor's stand was mem·o·ra·ble. They said, "Ob·vi·ous·ly, the pro·fes·sor was en·ti·tled to this grand o·pin·ion of his."

Learn to Spell 500 Words a Day by Camilia Sadik - O

 Copy these words and do not try to guess the spelling of words. Look at each word, use your eyes as cameras, and then copy it. Concentrate on the schwa sound of "o" when copying these words:

obtain	obvious	obnoxious	occur
offend	opinion	oppress	polite
philosophy	promote	propel	educator
inspector	provoke	solicit	professor
melody	memory	superior	interior
exterior	error	terror	governor
major	author	tailor	advisor
counselor	chancellor	councilor	tailor
favor	harbor	razor	rumor
doctor	color	donor	oppose
memorable	impotent	corporation	tomato

> Know that the **26** English letters produce over **90** sounds we call phonics, which are spelled in more than **180** ways we call spelling patterns.

Phonics-based Spelling Books for all Ages by Camilia Sadik

Book 1: *Learn to Spell 500 Words a Day* (6 volumes: A, E, I, O, U, Consonants)
Vowels are inconsistent, they rule English, and they cannot be avoided. In this book, each vowel is dissected and isolated in a volume. The eight consonants c, g, h, q, s, x, w, and y are also inconsistent; and they are isolated in a volume. Each lesson begins with a spelling rule, followed by a list of the words that follow that rule, followed by comprehensive and detailed practice lessons, and students are asked to read aloud to memorize the spelling of hundreds of words at a time. This book is for the intermediate level, ideal for grades 4-12 and for adult learners.

Book 2: *100 Spelling Rules*
Each spelling rule in this book is followed by a list of nearly all the words that follow it. Advanced students learn to spell hundreds of words from this book. Sadik's books are cumulative, and the book *100 Spelling Rules* is a book for the advance level.

Book 3: *Read Instantly* - A book to teach phonics
This book is to teach phonics, and in it lies the groundwork for learning the rules that govern phonics. Anyone capable of learning the ABC's is guaranteed to learn to read from this book. Each vowel is dissected and isolated in a chapter in the second half of this book. Parents can now teach reading before sending kids to schools. This book is for beginners, but all learners need to start with it to learn phonics in a brand-new way.

Book 4: *The Compound Words* - 7,000 Compound and Hyphenated Words
Unlike looking up words in a dictionary, over 5,000 compound words and 2,000 hyphenated words are isolated in this book, grouped alphabetically, colored, and prepared for adults and children to read and learn. As in "rustproof," a compound word is composed of two or more words. As in "face-to-face," a hyphenated word is made of the two or more words, separated by hyphens.

Book 5: *Teachers' Guide*
This guide is for teachers, parents, or adult learners. It contains explanations of the methodology and the symbols and concepts used in the books. It contains dyslexia solutions, spelling tests, and more. *Read more* → SpellingRules.com

How to purchase books by Camilia Sadik

SpellingRules.com   Amazon.com   Bookstores Worldwide

About the Author

Linguist Camilia Sadik spent 15 years intensely dissecting English, discovering over 100 spelling rules, applying the rules in 600 phonics-based spelling lessons, class-testing her discoveries and preparing learning books for children and adults to read and spell hundreds of words at a time. The 30 unique learning features in Sadik's book make learning to read and spell inescapable. Sadik worked hard to make spelling easy and possible for all ages and all types of learners. In addition, Sadik found an easy solution to end dyslexia in spelling and in writing letters in reverse. Learning to spell and slowing down to write words slowly ends dyslexia.

Sadik saw the details of English sounds and their various spelling patterns and used that in easy-to-use vowels and consonants books. See these examples:

The vowel **A** has 5 sounds that are spelled in 12 ways.

The vowel **E** has 7 sounds that are spelled in 17 ways.

The vowel **I** has 8 sounds that are spelled in 19 ways.

The vowel **O** has 12 sounds that are spelled in 20 ways.

The vowel **U** has 6 sounds that are spelled in 28 ways.

Eight **consonants** have 50 sounds that are spelled in 60 ways.

Academically, Sadik earned a BA in Philosophy from WSU and an MA in Applied Linguistics from SDSU. In addition, Sadik earned California Teaching Credentials and is certified in teaching ABE and ESL. Before writing books, Sadik spent over 10 years reading the best of the world's literature.

©1997 Camilia Sadik

All rights reserved. Camilia Sadik patented each new spelling rule she discovered. Printed in the United States of America, and except as permitted under the United States Copyright Act of 1976. No part of this publication may be reproduced or distributed in any form or by any means, or stored in a database retrieval system, without prior written permission of the publisher.

www.ingramcontent.com/pod-product-compliance
Lightning Source LLC
Chambersburg PA
CBHW060514300426
44112CB00017B/2668